AF539288

Michelangelo

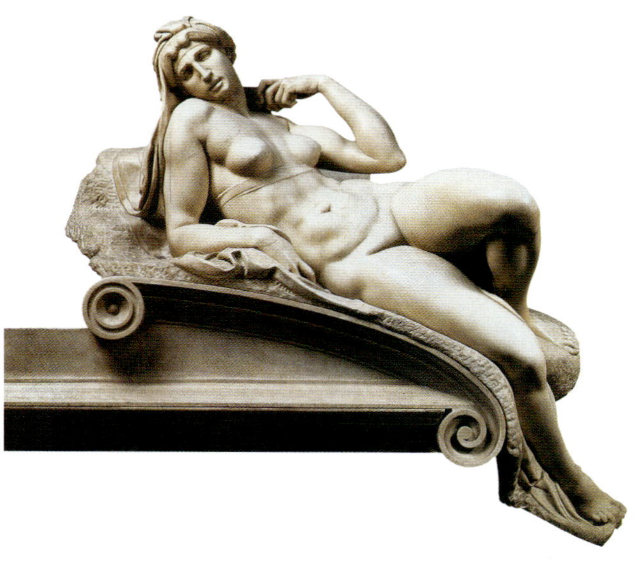

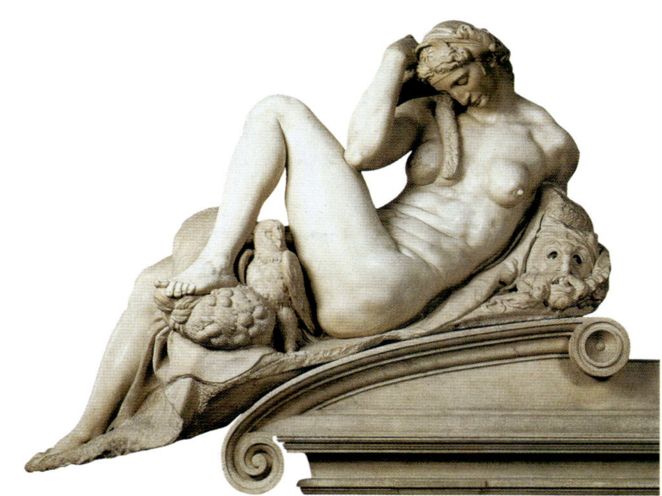

ISBN 1-84013-765-7

Published in 2005 by Grange Books
an imprint of Grange Book Plc
The Grange Kingsnorth Industrial Estate
Hoo, nr Rochester, Kent ME3 9ND
www.Grangebooks.co.uk

Printed in China

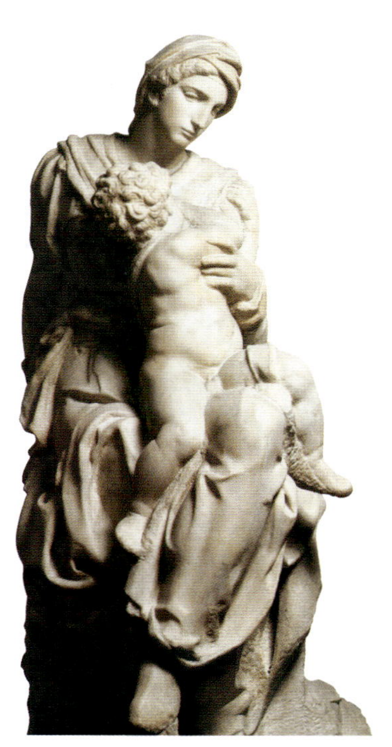

Michelangelo

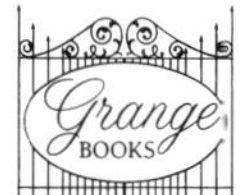

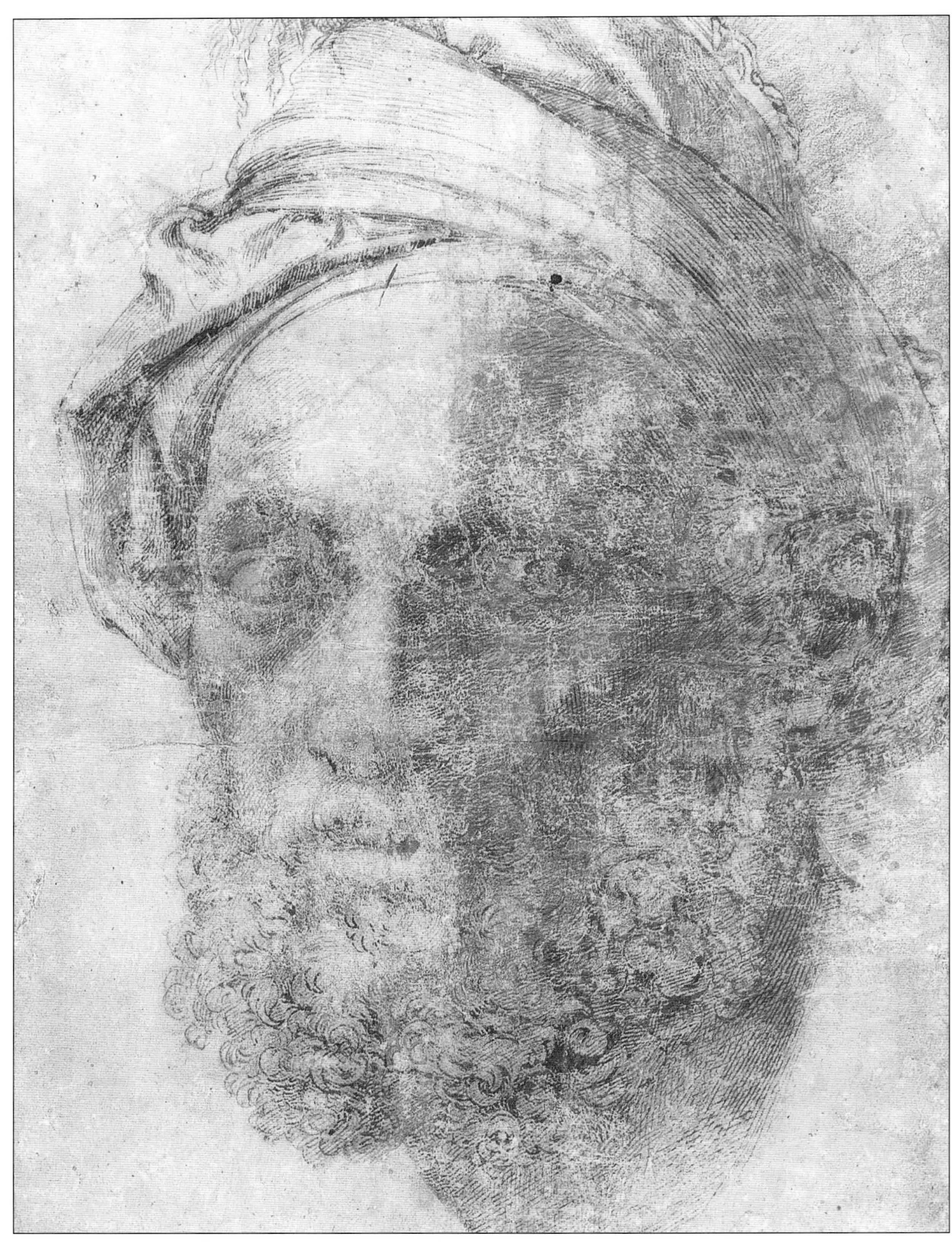

MICHELANGELO

The name "Michelangelo" has come to mean "genius". Firstly because his talents spanned sculpture, painting, architecture, army engineering and even poetry to the extent that he became the personification of original thinking and avant-garde esthetics. Secondly, he is the artist through whom Humanism found full expression.

In the Renaissance, Humanism was more an attitude and style of thinking than a doctrine. The focus was on Man, not abstract intellectual ideas. The key issues were: What does Man come from? Where does he belong in the Universe? What, indeed, is Man? Is perfection of this world? The answers were never final or dogmatic but open to analysis, debate and investigation. Humanism could mutate from Christian to Pagan, from secular to whatever.

Humanism took first root in Florence under leading Neo-Platonists such as Marsilio Ficino, Pico della Mirandola and Leonardo da Vinci. From there it spread throughout Europe. The powerful creativity, expressiveness and intensity of Michelangelo's works beautifully illustrate the Humanist conception of the world. To best understand the artist, we must begin with a look at his life.

Childhood

The close of the 15th century marked the start of a new era. Decades of plague, war and famine had thrown Europe into a period of radical change. Mindsets were changing. Medieval values were rejected as people with a deep need for social change looked to their flourishing economies and a range of new technologies. Lorenzo de Medici, François I and other great Europeans maintained that the arts were as important as war. Moreover, the printing press made culture more accessible to greater numbers of people. It was in these revolutionary times that a minor civil servant from the petty nobility of Florence was appointed local governor (*podestà*) of the diocese of Arezzo. His name was Lodovico di Leonardo Buonarroti Simoni and he settled in the town of Caprese. His second child, Michelangelo, was born on Sunday, March 6, 1475.

1. *Self Portrait with Turban* Quill, 36.5 x 25 cm. The Louvre, Paris.

After two terms as local governor, he moved the family back to their homestead in Settignano just outside Florence. When his wife died in 1492, he was left with five children to raise alone. Michelangelo was only six at the time. Left motherless, he became a tight-lipped, insolent and stubborn child. Packed off to board with a stonecutter's family, he soon channelled his frustration into extracting stone from the nearby quarry alongside his foster family's own children. Alongside them, Michelangelo learned the tools and skills of that he would later apply to his masterpieces. "If there's anything good in me, he told his friend Giorgio Vasari one day, it comes from being born in the subtle atmosphere of our Arezzo countryside, and, from my wet nurse's milk, I drew forth the hammer and chisel I use to make my statues", according to Robert Coughlan. Later in life, Michelangelo would see this experience as the true source of his art.

Michelangelo was to travel a path that diverged sharply from that of his brothers who went into the silk business. He stood out because of his fine intelligence and sensitivity. His father sent him to study under Francesco d'Urbino, a top grammarian who opened Michelangelo's eyes to the beauties of Renaissance art. But Michelangelo was always more inclined toward drawing than classical studies and he quickly made friends with an older co-student, Francesco Granacci, who was also a student of the painter Domenico Ghirlandaio. Struck by Michelangelo's ambition and drive, Granacci persuaded him to take up art too and even helped convince his father, who thought "manual labour" was unbecoming to the son of a Florentine civil servant. Michelangelo stood his ground and his father eventually relented, exploiting a distant kinship to the Medici to enroll him in Ghirlandaio's workshop (*bottega*) as an "apprentice or valet". Though he seethed at the thought of being anyone's valet, he kept silent. In any event, Michelangelo joined Ghirlandaio's workshop at the age of 13 on April 1, 1488. It was his first formal step toward becoming the greatest painter the Renaissance ever produced.

The Medici Factor

Domenico Ghirlandaio's workshop catered strictly to affluent Florentines. He had a flair for frescos and his paintings are among the earliest to show a Renaissance influence. He worked on the Sistine Chapel alongside Botticelli, Rosselli and Pinturicchio under the direction of Perugi and served as personal decorator to Lorenzo de Medici.

In drawing and painting classes at the workshop, Michelangelo's talent soon set him apart from his peers. On his own initiative, he did a colour version of a work of Schoen's. Ghirlandaio soon realized he had a genius on his hands and made him study Giotto, Masaccio and Santo Spirito. Altogether, Michelangelo spent three years in the atelier copying masters such as Donatello and Jacopo della Quercia, sharpening his eye as he went along. There, he became fully aware of his own visual acuity, analytical mindset and solid feel for colors. He also made enemies at the atelier, for many were envious, and his nose bore the mark of a blow by the jealous, violent Torrigiani, to whom we owe the Villa Romana.

Though he met Lorenzo de Medici through Ghirlandaio, Michelangelo would always deny that his teacher had taught him anything of value or influenced him in any way. Filled with ambition, Michelangelo was sure of his exceptional talent and liked to see it as the sole reason for his success.

It was a good era for artists. Lorenzo de Medici, also known as "Il Magnifico", was a patron of art and literature who, inside his own palace, founded a school chaired by Bertoldo, a student of Donatello's, then prominent in the Florence art scene. The most promising young artists flocked to study sculpture there. Through that school, Michelangelo met the Medici family and was greatly impressed by their fabulous collection of sculptural works. The school marked a quantum leap in his artistic education and led to a lifelong working relationship with the Medici family.

Michelangelo became a symbol of the Renaissance, with innovative output that contrasted sharply with that of his predecessors – from whom he drew unparalleled inspiration nonetheless. He had found his calling: sculpture! The outstanding quality of his output quickly caught the eye of Lorenzo de Medici, who promoted his reputation and secured his introduction into high society. There, Michelangelo met other art patrons, fellow artists, key statesmen and prominent Humanists who frequented the Court of Florence. Lorenzo's two sons, Giovanni and Giulio, were two of these acquaintances and they were to assume special significance through long hours of study and leisure spent together. Many years later, they would become the popes Leo X and Clement VII and commission Michelangelo's greatest masterpieces.

Homecoming and Travel

By age 16, Michelangelo's many works included *The Battle of the (Lapiths and) Centaurs*, an allusion to the sarcophagi of Late Antiquity, and *The Madonna of the Stairs*, two base reliefs now at the Casa Buonarroti in Florence. But 1492 brought upheaval to the young master's life. Lorenzo de Medici died, paving the way for the Apocalypse-haranguing prior Girolamo Savonarola to help drive the incapable Piero de Medici and other heirs from the city. Michelangelo left for home in Settignano. Though still only semi-schooled in both painting and carving, he had already shown clear artistic skills and inimitable originality. As a person, Michelangelo was often called vain, asocial, taciturn, irritable, overbearing and impetuous. Convinced of his genius, he saw himself as a professional artist rather than a student. During his stay at home, he painted *Hercules*, first owned by the Strozzi family before passing on to François I and later disappearing. Michelangelo then went off to Venice in a disappointing search for inspiration. Moving on to Bologna, he became a protégé of Francesco Aldobrandi and completed several statuettes for the *Reliquary* of San Domenico church, a work left unfinished by Nicolo da Pisa in the 13th century. As city councillor and old friend of Lorenzo de Medici, Aldobrandi gave Michelangelo his first real commission that included a statue of Saint Petronus, completion of a second Saint Petronus holding a scale model of the city in his hands and most important, the *Angel Candelabra* to counterbalance the first two. In particular, this last work offers striking proof of the breadth of the young artist's techniques and sense of esthetics, from the generous bulging muscles, incisively chiseled drapery and gentle facial features. Around 1495, Michelangelo returned to Florence, now a republic free of Piero de Medici. Thanks to the pro-republican Lorenzo di Pierfrancesco de Medici, Michelangelo carved a *Sleeping Cupid*, possibly the one now on display at the Art Academy of Mantua. Amusingly, Lorenzo suggested artificially aging the cupid to fetch a better price from Cardinal Riario di San Giorgio. And Michelangelo did so! Hardly fooled, the cardinal knew quality when he saw it and invited the artist to Rome. Thus began Michelangelo's first period in Rome where he could explore even more of the splendors of the Antiquity he had first tasted in the Medici gardens. This experience only heightened his passion for that style. Here he did *Bacchus*, his first major work and one of a few of purely Pagan inspiration. Most of his commissions would come from the Catholic Church, then omnipotent across Europe. In 1497, he finished *La Pietà* (*The Rome Pietà*), one of his most beautiful accomplishments. It was commissioned by the French ambassador to the Vatican under King Charles VIII, Cardinal Jean de la Grolaye de Villiers (Jean de Bilhères de Lagraulas) for his own tomb. Now in St. Peter's Basilica in Rome, it is the perfect depiction of God's sacrifice and inner beauty. Michelangelo was now 22; his youth was not a string of art classes, a budding track record of esthetic boldness and timeless artwork.

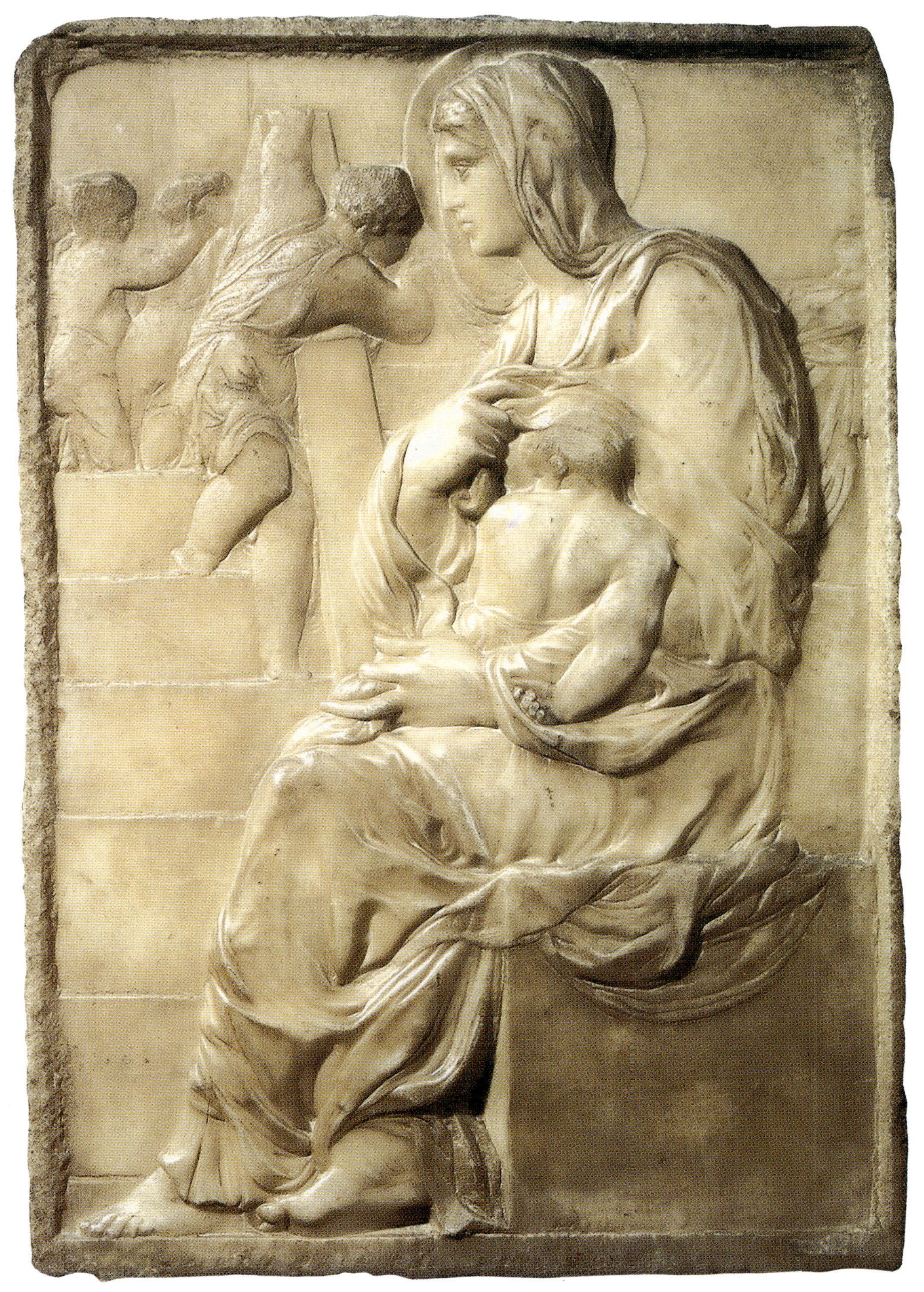

2. *Madonna of the Stairs*, circa 1490. Marble, 55.5 x 44 cm. Casa Buonarroti, Florence.

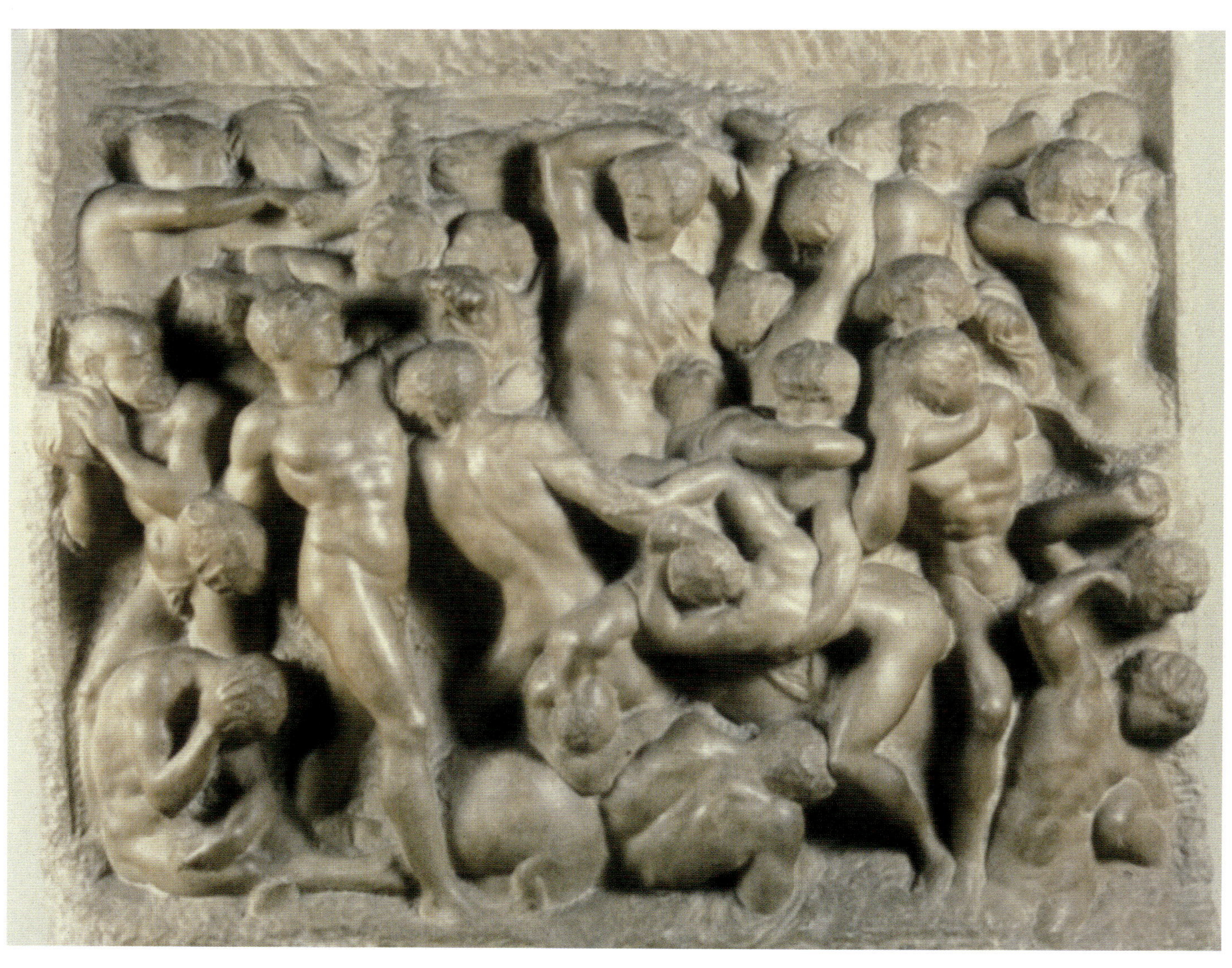

Inner Tension

His greatest battles lay within: How do you go from mind to matter when your mind is in constant motion, pressuring for ever more evolution of style and activity with changing demands? His first works revealed inner anguish that would only grow with time. First of all, this was a time when artists, then closely tied to the guilds, were being coopted into the cosmopolitan and cultivated spheres of the elite. This elite became active art patrons, trend-setting fashion designers and intellectual activists. They started networking with figurative painters, architects, philosophers and other intellectuals. Thus, the social role of creative thinkers changed substantially: art shifted from a medium for a spiritual or philosophical message to a tool that served a religious, political or business objective.

Secondly, Michelangelo's anguish intensified because he was split between Christianity and Paganism: the most ambitious and unbounded of Renaissance artists to depict the Catholic faith was a Pagan. After all, doesn't the Jesus in Michelangelo's *Last Judgment* in the Sistine Chapel bear a mild resemblance to Zeus? Through its innate power and vitality, the work transcends the stiffness and insipidness of Evangelical compassion. Yet the *Pietà Dolorosa* of San Marco in Rome is so richly Christian in its compassion, pain and sacrifice to God. Significantly, it is the only work Michelangelo ever signed showing the Holy Virgin in the seated position, with the limp body of her son against her womb along an almost horizontal axis. They are both presented as very vulnerably human and Michelangelo wastes no paint underscoring this fact. He skips the bleeding wounds – after all, why trivialize the event? The way Mary holds Jesus gives the divine oeuvre its sublime expression of God's sacrifice for man's salvation – the gift of His son. The work interweaves the absolute certainty of Resurrection, God's forgiveness and the sweet splendour of Heaven. This is what the artist saw and what his hand has bequeathed.

Michelangelo became one of the most influential artists of his era. Nicknamed "Il Divino", his genius moved art forward by drawing inspiration from Antiquity and reshaping it for the greater glorification of Man. The apogee of Michelangelo's youth was his 4.34 meter *David* in marble, now at the Accademia of Florence. First sketched in 1501, it was completed in 1504. This hero of the Old Testament is a hulk of naked muscle and pensive determination shown alone sizing up his far more massive adversary – it was a break with tradition to show David without Goliath's head in hand. Instead, Michelangelo selected the moment of truth before the action rather than the deed itself: he captures the inner dimension of the event. Thus *David* epitomizes the invincibility of the Republic of Florence. And it was placed in front of the Palazzo Vecchio, the seat of government. It was plain proof to his contemporaries, artist and citizen alike, that Michelangelo had risen above the crowd to become the best of artists, for he had enriched the beauty of gracefully pure lines with stunning internalisation and expressiveness.

3. *Battle of the Centaurs*, 1492. Marble, 80.5 x 88 cm. Casa Buonarroti, Florence.

The Da Vinci Factor

Michelangelo could not escape the thrust of Leonardo Da Vinci's new trends, and his sense of esthetics changed when the final sketch for Da Vinci's *Saint Anne* went on display in Florence. Commenting on the work, he admitted it was "a new way of interpreting the relationship between the characters, expressed through powerful masses and the space they occupy."

Florence was a free country, and the Medici were out of power. Florentines wanted to depict the city's history in all its magnificence. Da Vinci was one natural choice to represent what the Republic of Florence wanted to promote. He was commissioned for a fresco, in the Sala del Gran Consiglio of the Palazzo Vecchio, depicting the Battle of Anghiari between Florence and Milan in 1434. Michelangelo then joined the fray with a commission for a fresco of the *Battle of Cascina*. Neither was ever finished.

Both infuriated and influenced by Da Vinci, Michelangelo was developing answers to an esthetic issue of his own: how do you isolate a human figure in a volume of space to best express the quest for universality? Their rivalry was great. In addition to an age difference of 23 years, Da Vinci was the rational scientist while Michelangelo was a blend of spiritual and earthy. Tension mounted into open rivalry. One day Da Vinci was invited to join a chat on Dante as he was walking by the Santa Trinità church. Then Michelangelo came by and the old master asked him for his opinion. Michelangelo told him to answer the question himself for he had sketched a horse for Francesco Sforza that he didn't know how to cast in bronze as required. It did not endear the talented upstart in Da Vinci's eye as time would show.

Setting explanations aside, Michelangelo was obviously a brave and ambitious loner. As he said himself: "The greatest danger for most of us is not failure to reach too high a goal, but that we aim too low and reach that goal."

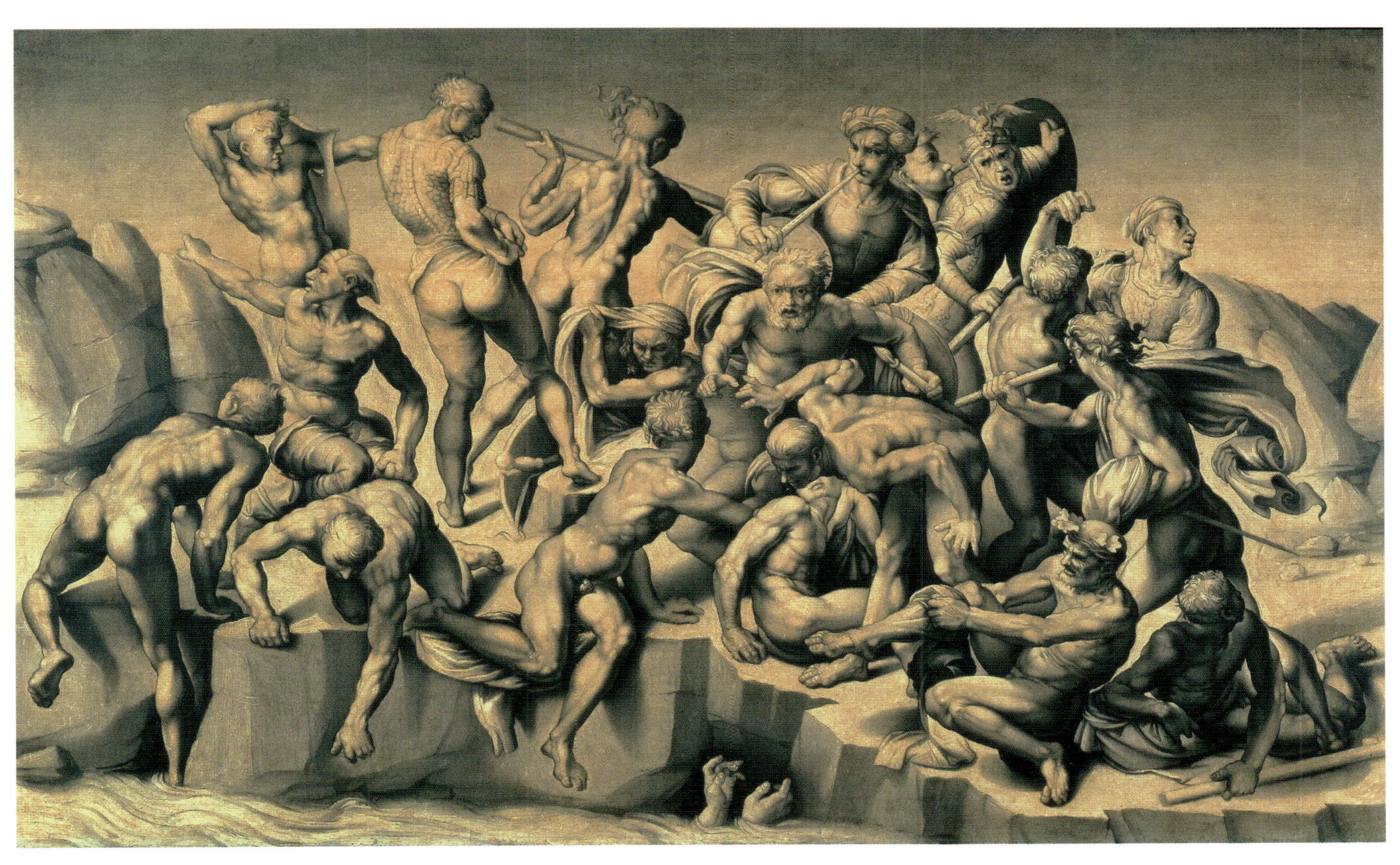

4. Antonio da Sangallo, *The Battle of Cascina* adapted from Michelangelo, circa 1542. Oil on panel. Private collection, Norfolk.

The Unprecedented Sculptor

Michelangelo's childhood and studious youth are perhaps the reasons behind the important place of sculpture in his works. As a child, his wet nurse was the wife of a stonecutter, so stone and chisel were handy, natural toys to him. And he enjoyed tracing his creativity back to the quarries. Another milestone was Michelangelo's visit to the San Marco gardens in the Medici Palace. Here he mixed with a wide range of Humanists and realized the artistic rewards of audacity, impetuosity and open-mindedness. Finally, he discovered the treasures of Antiquity that would nourish him with lifelong inspiration.

Michelangelo, on his own, advanced beyond the influence of his masters and developed his own clear ideas about what constituted a good sculptor. For example, he grasped that a mastery of human anatomy was an absolute prerequisite to fine sculpture and broke the taboo during that period on human dissection. From the prior of the Santo Spirito hospital, he obtained permission to study unclaimed corpses. However illegal the experience and detrimental to his health at times, Michelangelo thought it essential and even took pride in it. He openly bragged of the precision it added to the lines he reproduced. However great his talents in drawing, painting and architecture, he was drawn to art because of sculpture, and sculpture established his fame.

The young Michelangelo had a strong tendency to break the rules of art and force it to evolve. And he was not alone: Bertoldo di Giovanni's bronze works ranked just as high in Florence at the time – his teacher, Donatello, even called him "the greatest sculptor of the Early Renaissance, the driving force behind the evolution of sculpture". Thanks to these two artists, a new concept of the role of art, inspired by Donatello, came to the fore. Art was no longer expected to serve religious or other purposes – art was for beauty. It existed only to be admired, collected and exhibited. Michelangelo was to subscribe to that view for the rest of his life and he convinced his patron Lorenzo de Medici also.

In his flight from Florence, Michelangelo headed for Venice where Gianfrancesco Aldovrandri had him carve three statuettes in 1494 missing from the tomb of St. Dominic in Bologna. Rome too was to exert a lasting impact on the young artist. Sure of his future there, Michelangelo also appreciated its value as a source of great knowledge. Large-scale diggings there were continually unearthing priceless ancient masterpieces. Their monumental scale impressed him all the more as his genius delved ever further into Eternal Rome.

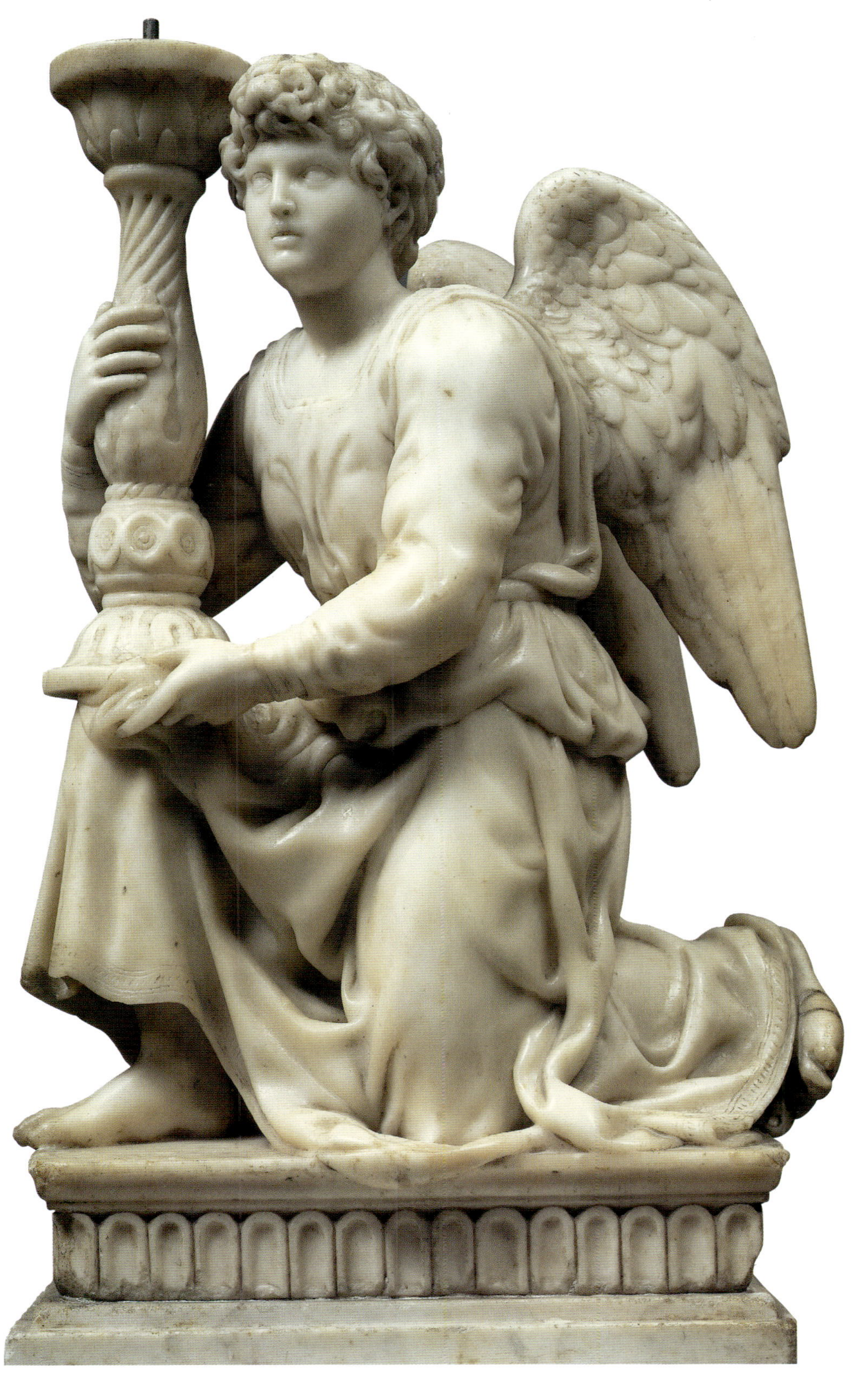

5. *Angel holding a candelabra,* 1495. Marble. Church of San Domenico, Bologna.

Soon a protégé of banking magnate Jacopo Galli, Michelangelo completed several major works, the first of which was the commission for *Bacchus*, now in the National Museum of Florence. Galli then secured him a commission from Cardinal Jean de la Grolaye de Villiers. Worth 450 ducats, the work was slated for the left transept of a sanctuary for the kings of France – the as yet unbuilt St. Denis Basilica outside Paris. Setting to work in 1498, Michelangelo would devote two years to one of the most famous works of our day: the *Pietà*.

When he returned to Florence, Michelangelo had been away for five years. The new republic had restored the level of law and order that had previously made it a haven for artistic thought and creativity. He got a hero's welcome. To symbolize the city's rebirth, he was commissioned to execute the monumental *David* in 1501. The achievement of so original and incisive a work cost him three years of work and pain. Again, Michelangelo discarded convention and astutely represented the tragic hero in a state of potential alert for victory under Divine protection, with only an elbow to protect a right flank otherwise entirely exposed to Evil.

In November 1503, Pope Pius III died, ceding the papal throne to Giuliano della Rovere, son of Lorenzo de Medici, who took the name Julius II. The new pope had fascinated Michelangelo since the days they shared in the Medici gardens. His Holiness persuaded Michelangelo to return to Rome where he commissioned a majestic tomb for himself along with other monuments. The artist wanted two slaves at the foot of the tomb and their story is as strange as their beauty. In short, they were never finished, never used for the tomb and Michelangelo ended up giving them away to his friend, Roberto Strozzi. Because of ironclad contracts governing commissions at the time, unfinished works were commonplace. They are also particularly common to Michelangelo because of his exceedingly high standards of excellence and quest for perfection.

In 1515 and 1516, he worked on his *Moses*, now at Rome's church of San Pietro in Vincoli, where it stands as the centerpiece of the final version of the tomb of Julius II. With influences from Classicism, it ranks among works the artist intended as monumental and representative of all the power and sensual delight that gives marble its unique nobility among stones. Rising 2.35 metres high, it shows the muscular patriarch seated, with the Ten Commandments under his right arm.

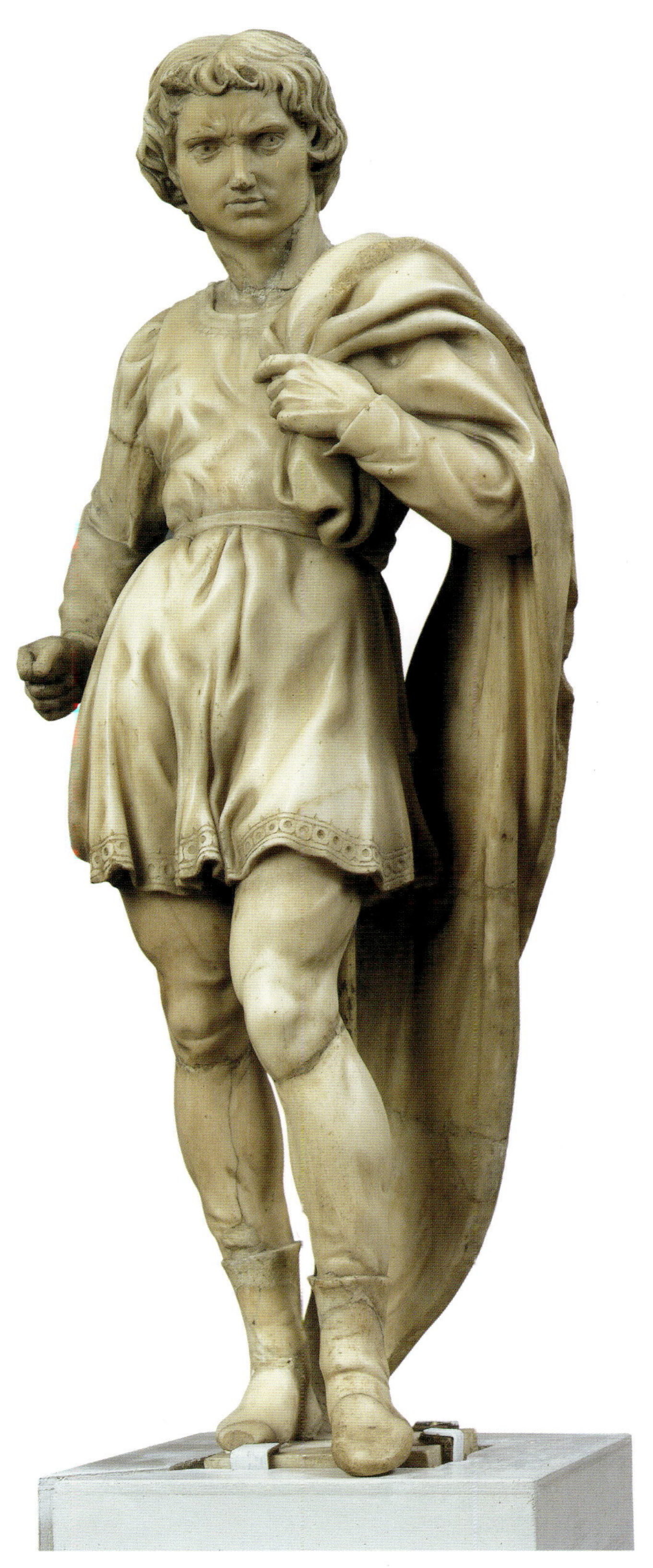

6. *Saint Proculus,* from the arca of San Domenico, 1495. Marbre. Church of San Domenico, Bologna.

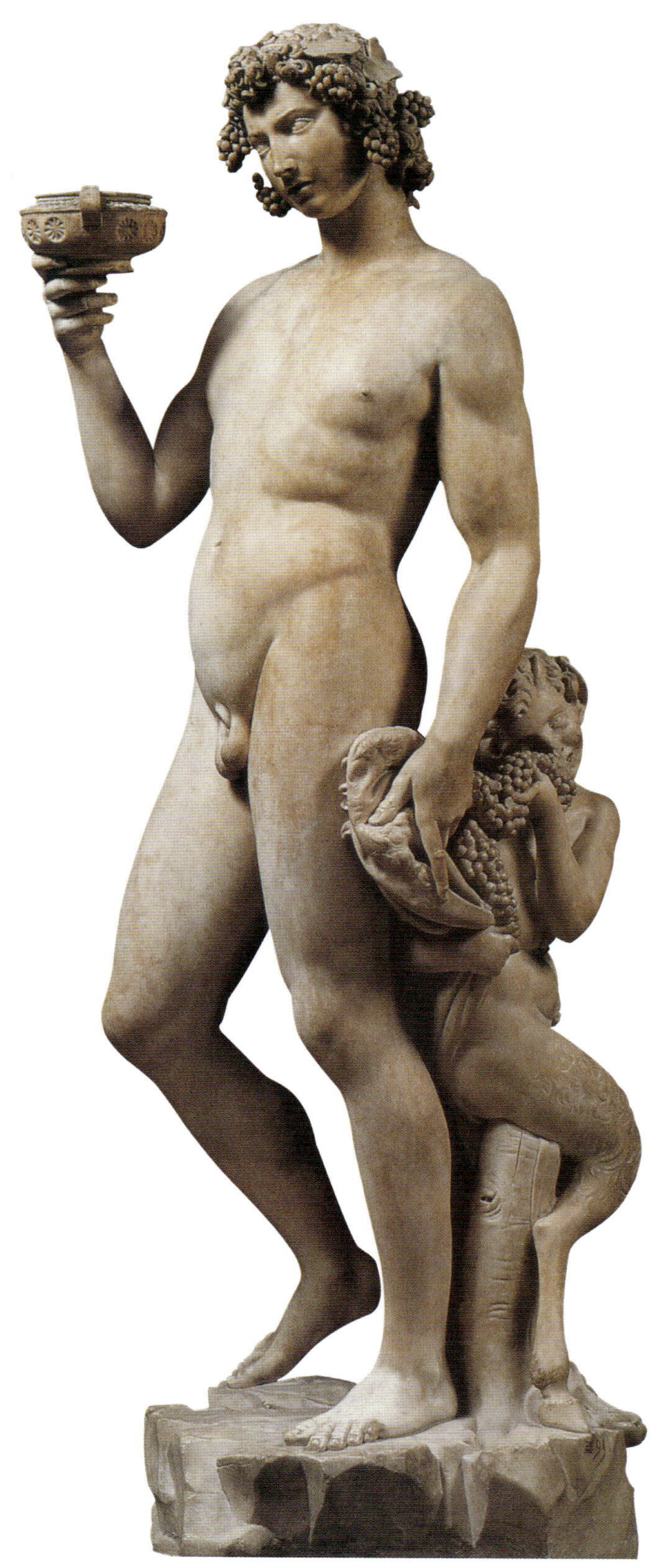

7. *Bacchus,* 1496-1497.
Marble, 203 cm.
Bargello, Florence.

8. *Pietà,* 1498-1499.
Marble, 174 cm.
St. Peter's, Vatican.

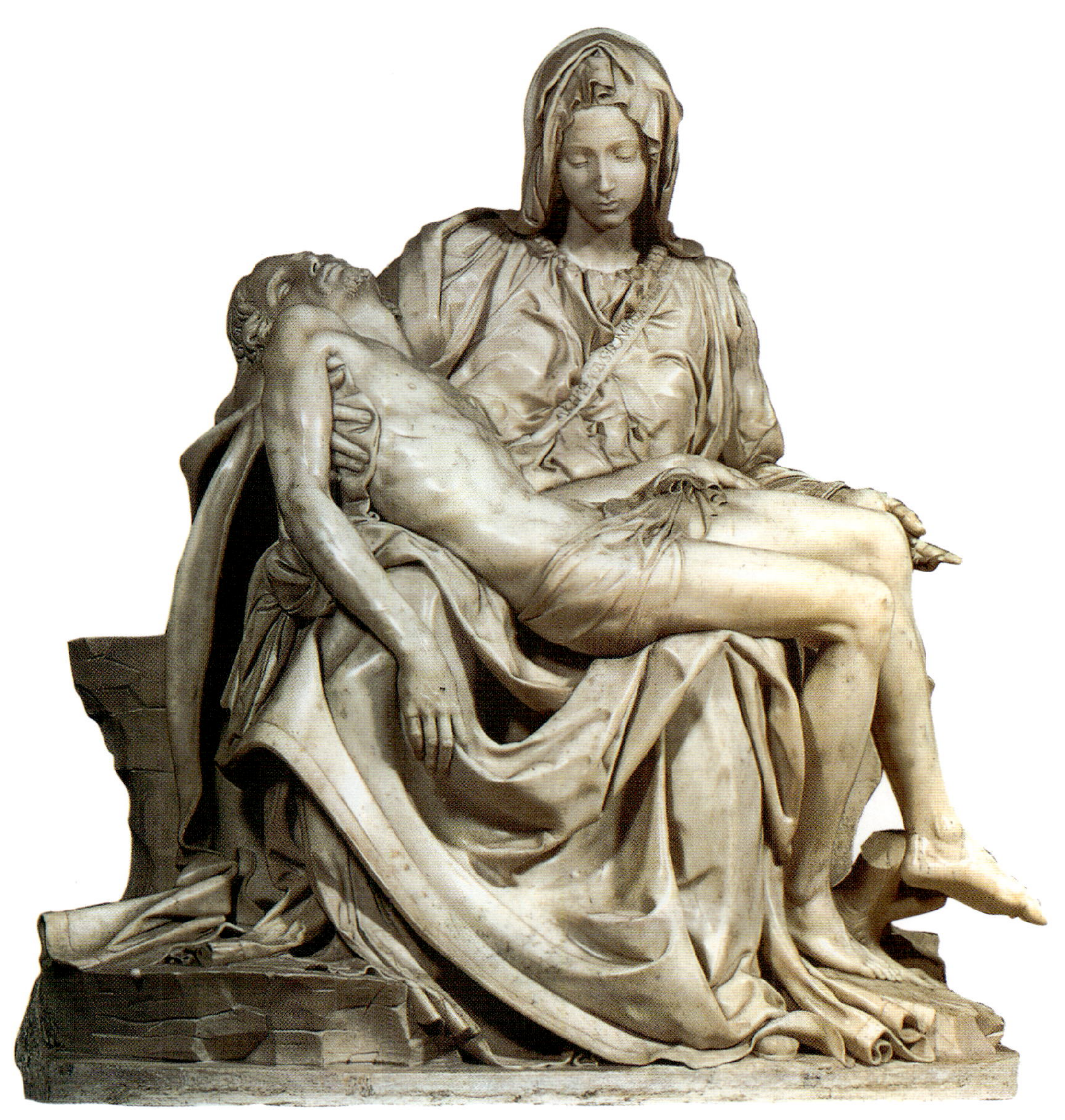

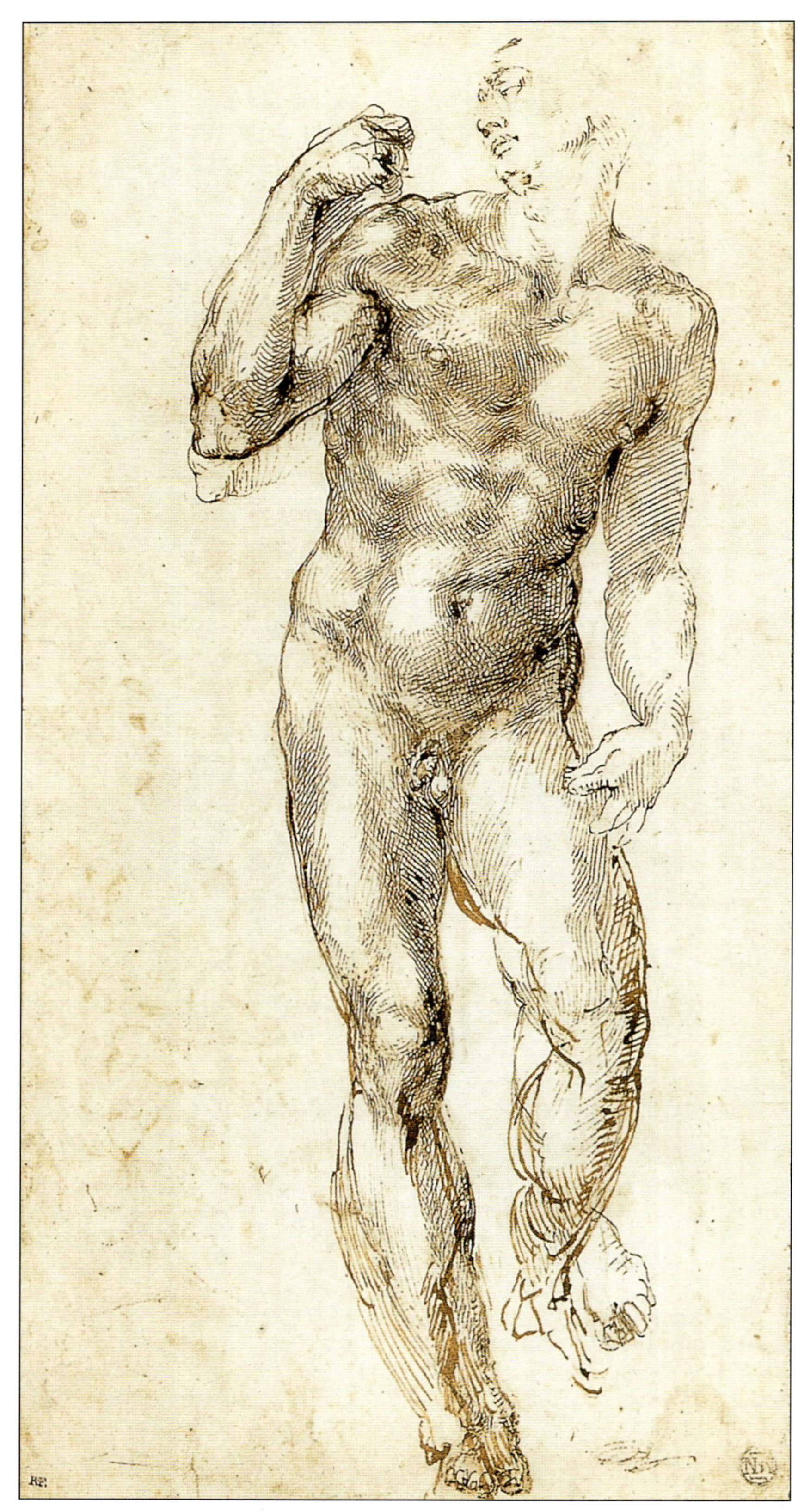

9. Sketch for a *David with Catapult,* 1501. Exhibition Room, The Louvre, Paris.

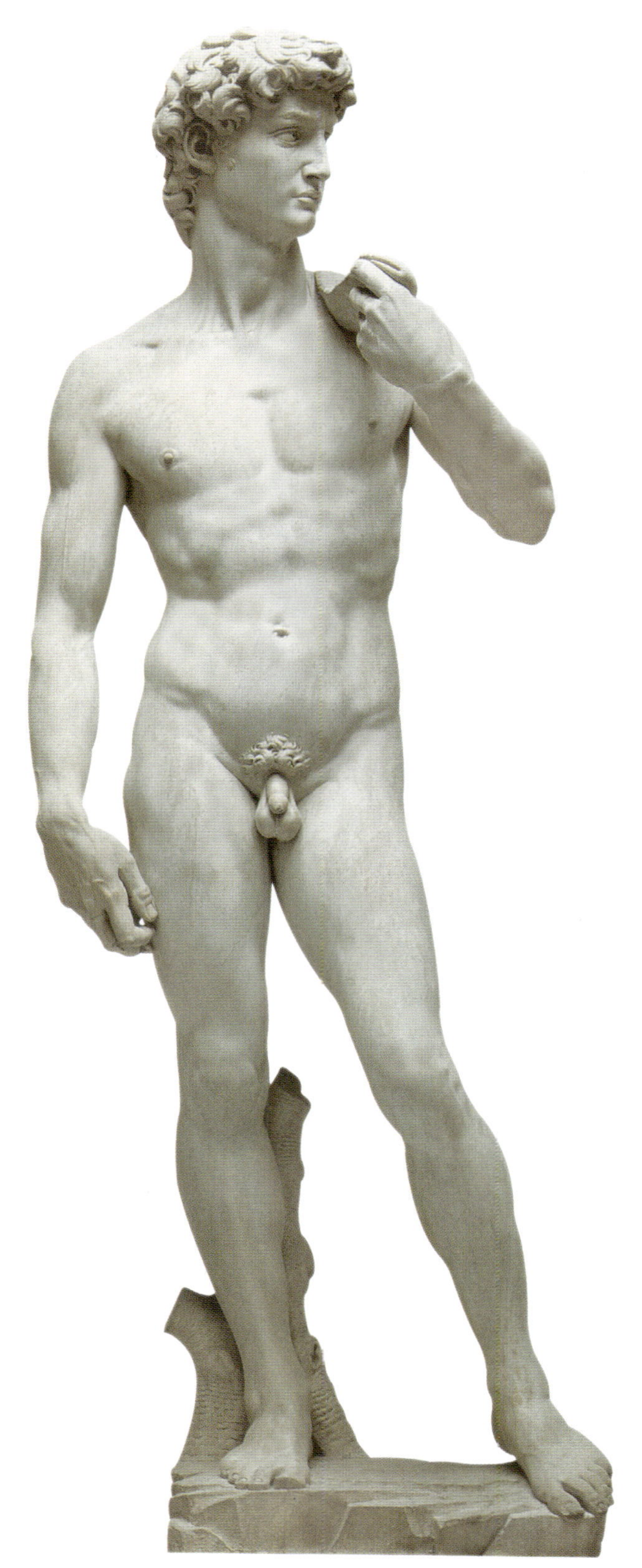

10. *David,* 1501-1504.
Marble, 410 cm.
Galleria
dell'Academia,
Florence.

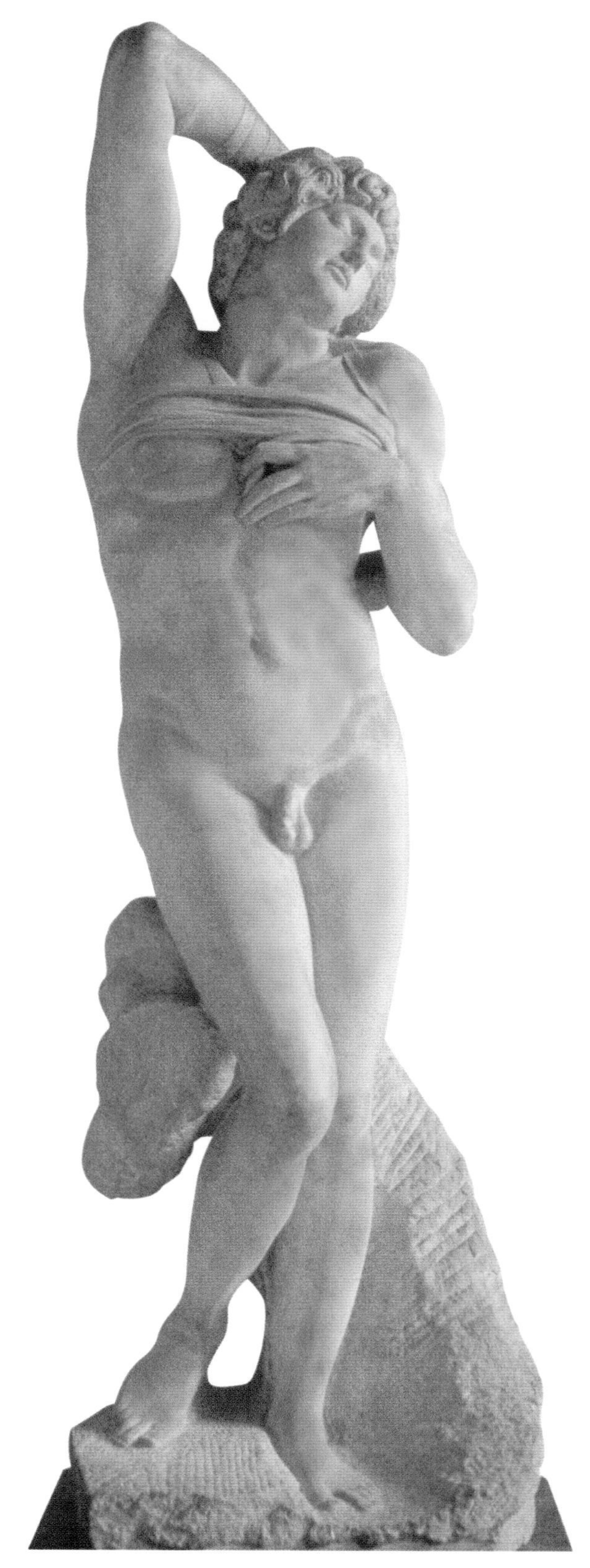

11. *The Dying Slave,*
1513-1516.
Marble, 229 cm.
The Louvre, Paris.

12. *The Rebellious Slave,*
1513-1516.
Marble, 229 cm.
The Louvre, Paris.

13. *Saint Matthew*,
1505-1506.
Marble, 271cm.
Galleria dell'Academia,
Florence.

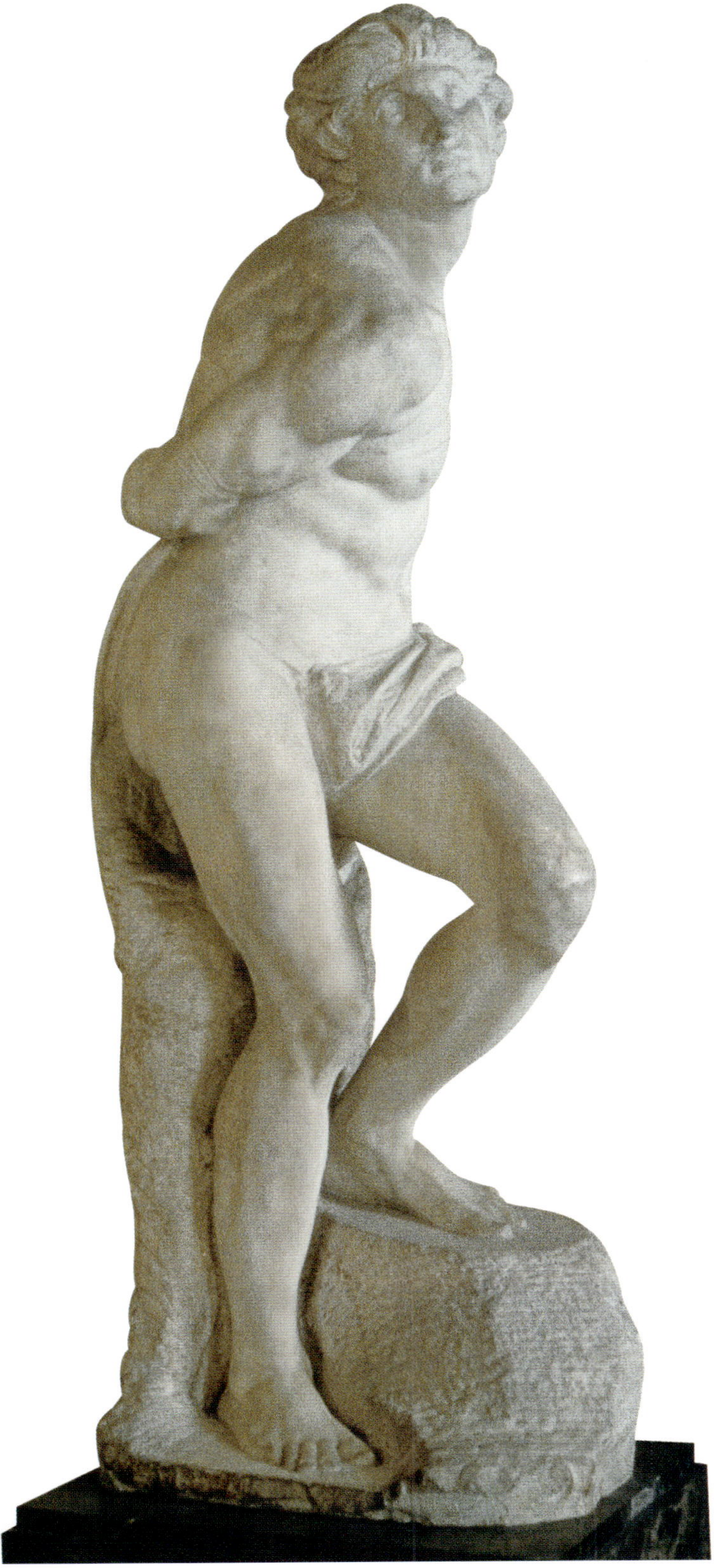

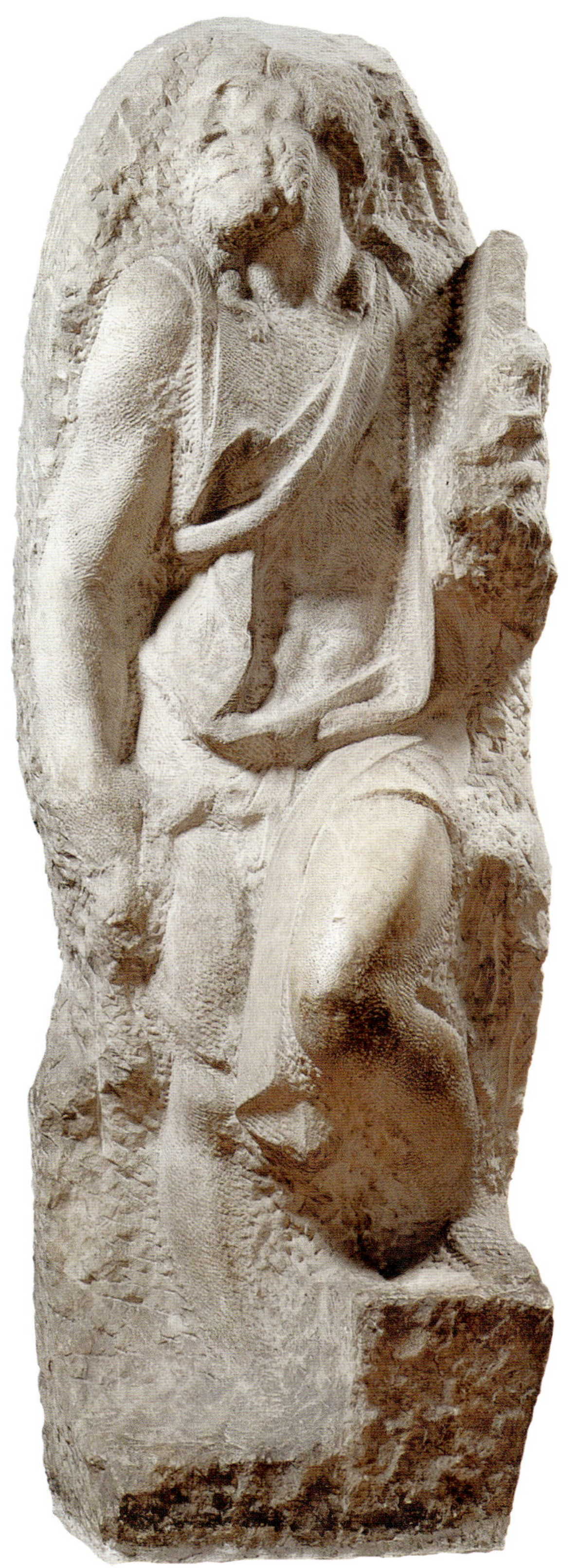

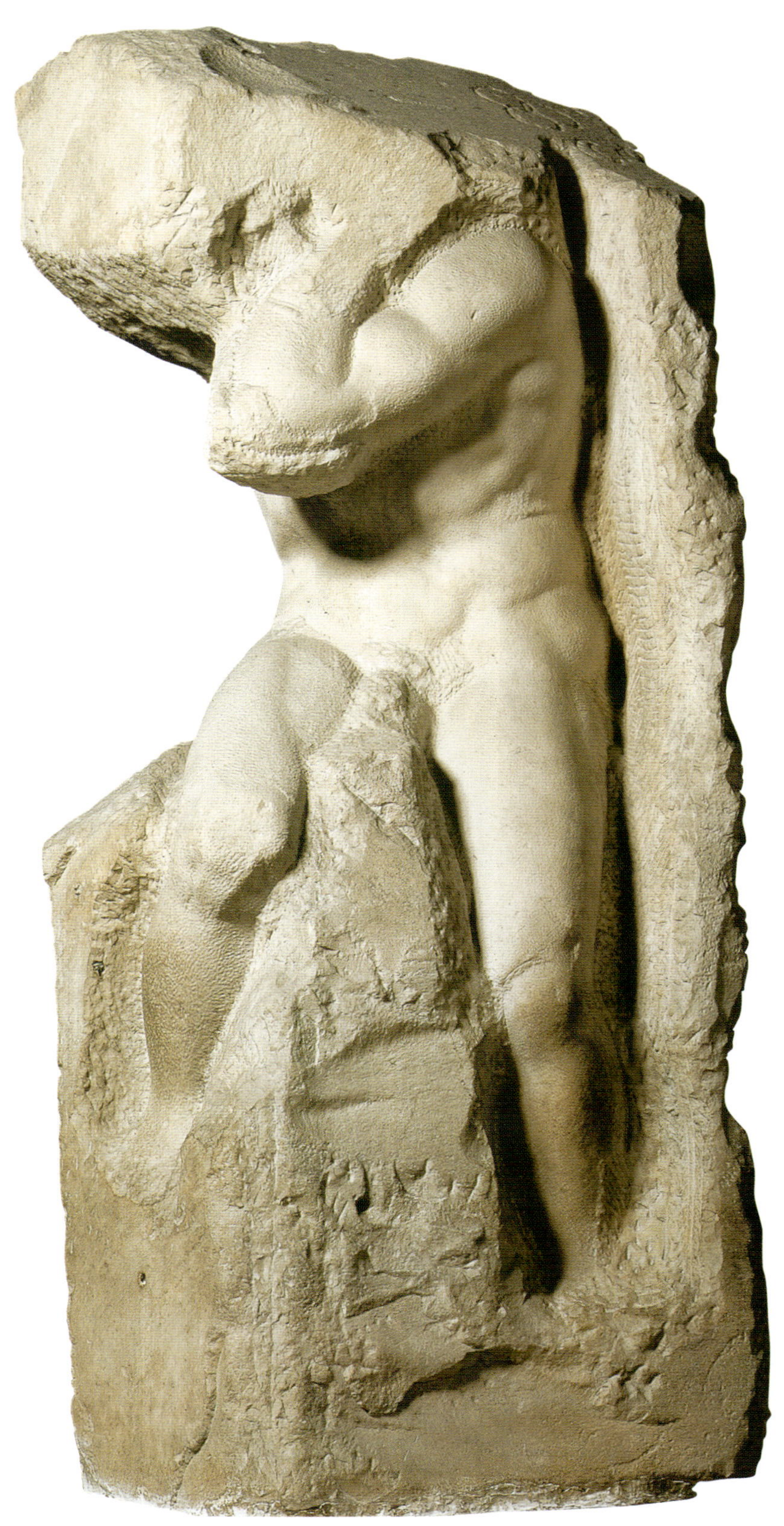

14. *Slave, Named Atlas*, 1519. Marble, 277 cm. Galleria dell'Academia, Florence.

Yet the tomb of Julius II does not herald a new period in the artist's work. Rather, it represents a main theme in an approach which would last almost four decades. The work is called *Tragoedia della Sepultura*. He began it with a trip to Carrara where he spent almost a year extracting blocks of marble that he cut up for easier shipping and handling. Problems soon arose when the pope became impatient with Michelangelo's inability to do one job at a time.

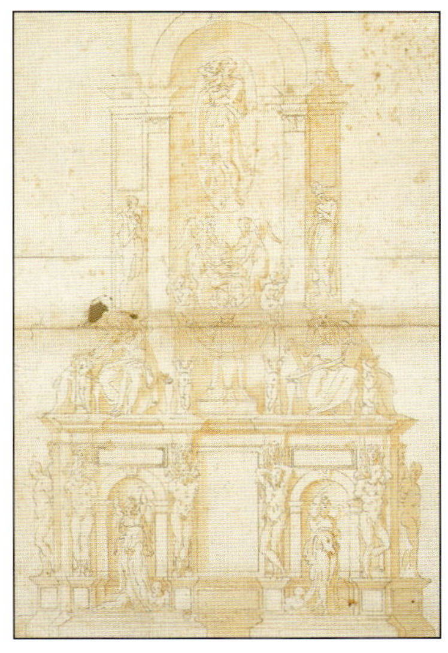

Moreover, Michelangelo had wages to pay at the quarry. Though the pope had promised him an open-door access to the Vatican, the artist's enemies were hardly idle in his absence. Doors were closing, and an irate Michelangelo stomped back to Florence where he found the authorities sympathetic to his piecemeal work habits.

By 1512, Julius II death was near and asked Michelangelo to complete the tomb in all haste. However, the artist's still growing reputation had swamped him with commissions. Work fell behind schedule, leaving the tomb unfinished when Julius died the following year. With the pope's heirs, Michelangelo negotiated a new contract for a scaled-back version of the original project over seven years for 16,500 ducats, then an enormous sum for him. The next pope, Leo X, never discovered how to handle Michelangelo and preferred to deal through the more straightforward Raphael. The result was that Michelangelo's talent became ensnarled in endless requirements for modifications.

Finally completed in 1547, the tomb of Julius II faithfully reflects the pope's love of Antiquity. It drew inspiration from the pope's collection of ancient statues in the Belvedere Gardens of the Vatican. Beside Moses stand Leah and Rachel to represent the active and contemplative facets of living an active Christian life.

Meanwhile, Michelangelo was also carving marble for the Medici family tombs in Florence. The work was important enough for Pope Clement VII to pardon Michelangelo for defending the city against the Medici so that he could honour the commission. In his Bull of 21 November 1531, the pope even commanded Michelangelo under pain of excommunication to complete the tombs and San Lorenzo Chapel.

As of 1512, the Republic of Florence was dead and the Medici were back in power. They embarked on new works of magnificence and Michelangelo took up the challenge by redoing the façade of the San Lorenzo church, the Medici funerary chapel. But work was halted in 1518 and the façade remains unfinished to this day.

15. Giacomo Rochetti, *Painting after the project of Michelangelo for the tomb of Pope Julius II*, 1513. Quill and ink, 52.5 x 39 cm. Staatliche Museum, Berlin.

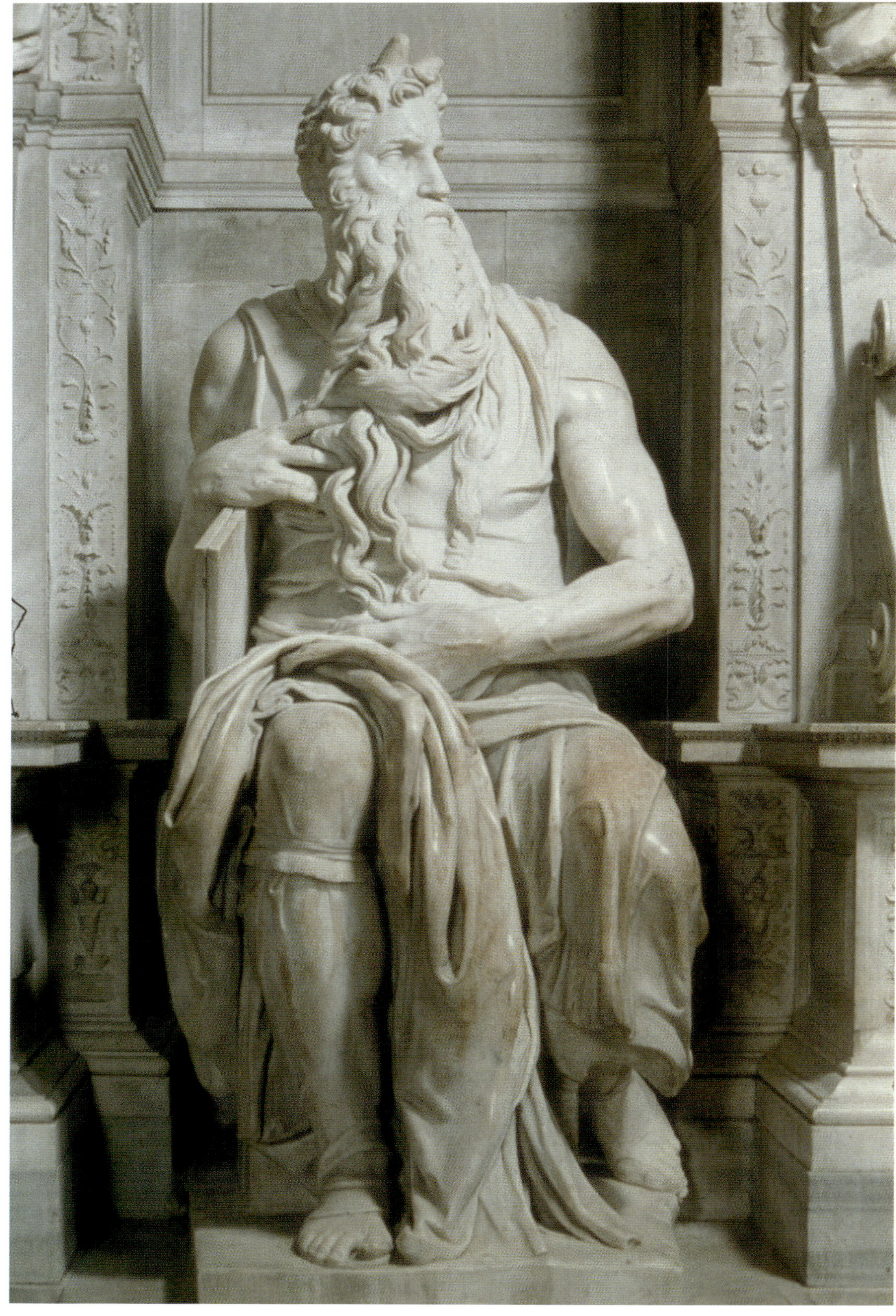

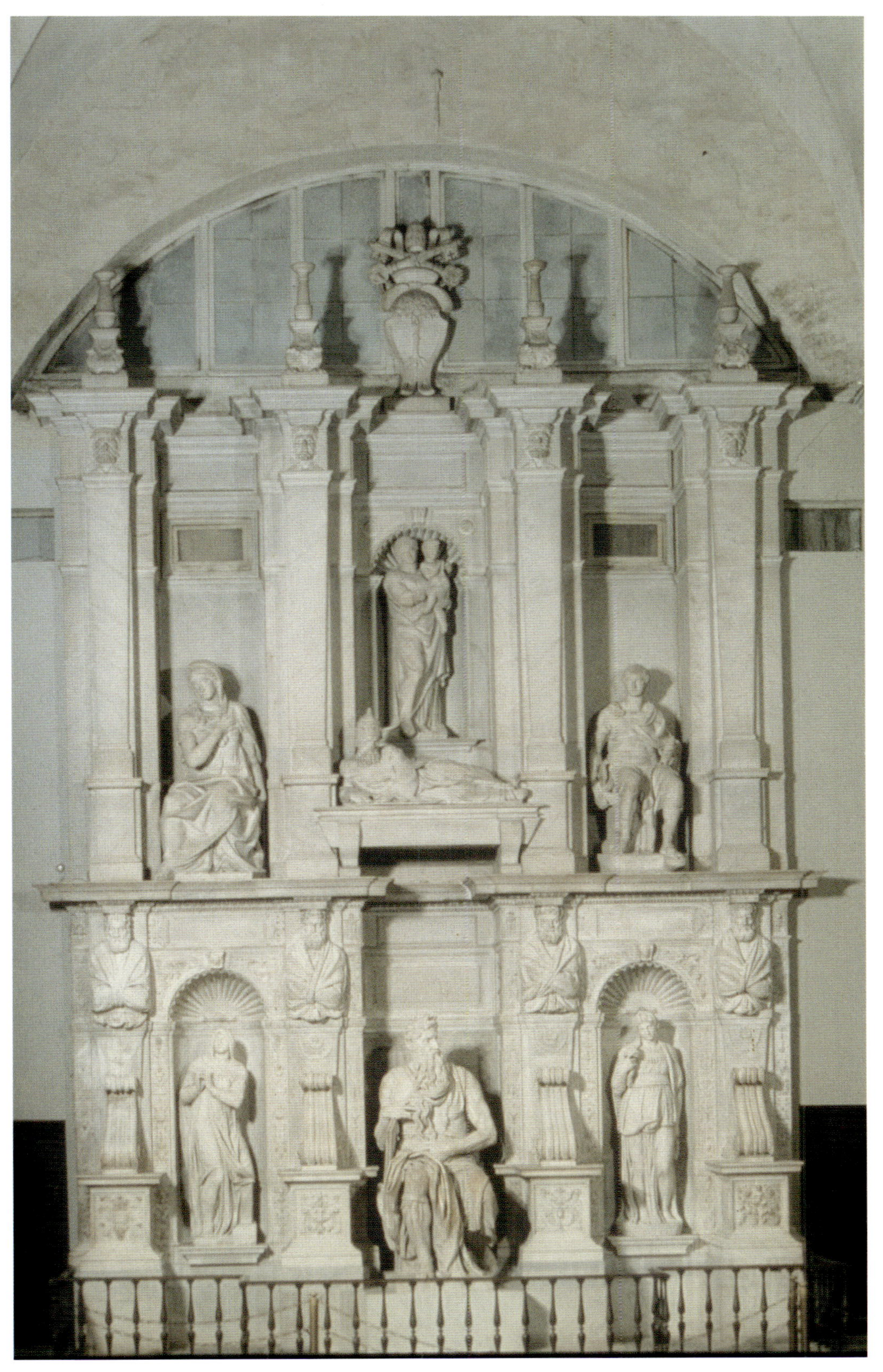

16. *Moses,* 1513-1515.
Marble, 235 cm.
Tomb of Pope Julius
II, San Pietro in
Vincoli, Rome.

17. *The Tomb of Pope
Julius II,* 1505-1545.
Marble, 263 x 156 cm.
San Pietro in Vincoli,
Rome.

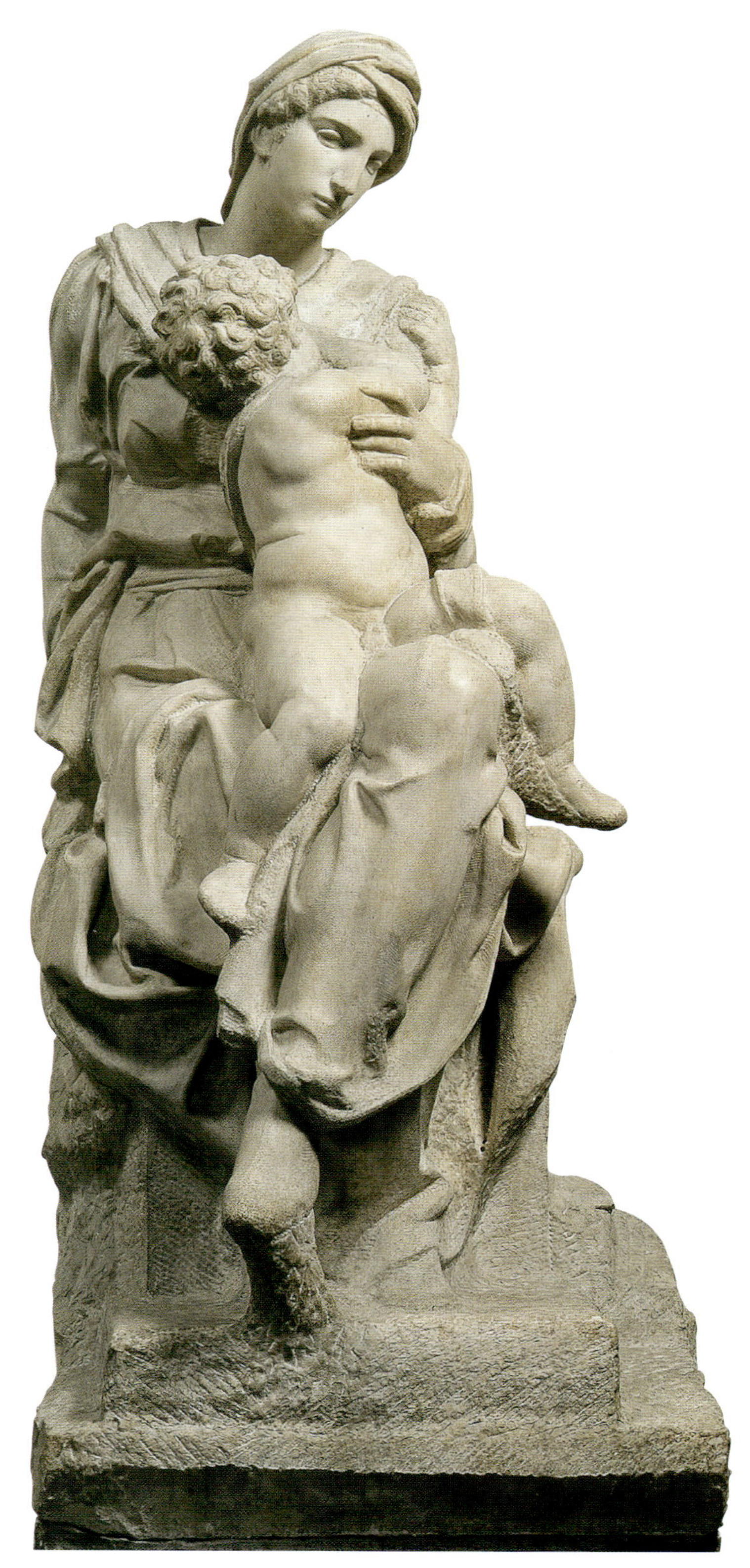

18. *Virigin and Child,*
1524-1534.
Marble, 226 cm.
Medici Chapel, San
Lorenzo, Florence.

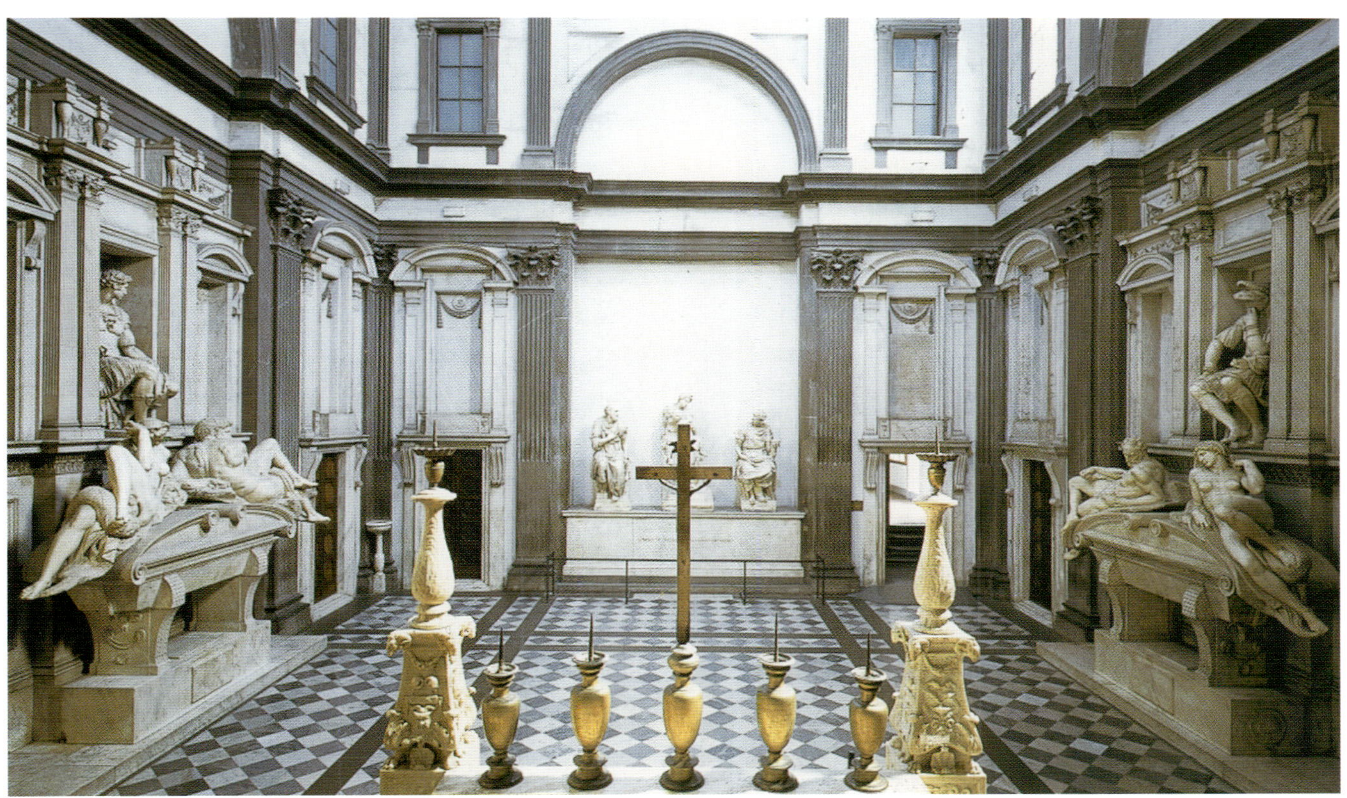

This architectural gem contains the tombs of Giuliano de Medici, Duke of Nemours, and Lorenzo, Duke of Urbino, the work spanning 1526 to 1534 and 1525 to 1527 respectively. Each boasts sensual, highly detailed sculptural elements, rich in allegorical content such as the *Night* and *Day* on Julius' tomb and the *Dusk* (*Twilight*) and *Dawn* on Lorenzo's tomb.

On the altar wall, there is also his beautiful, dynamic *Madonna and Child*, produced between 1521 and 1524. It shows Mary pulling the Infant Jesus towards her with a single hand. Full-featured, her face expresses sadness yet the lines remain supple, radiating serenity and patience with a touch of nostalgia, for she seems already aware of the joyous yet tragic destiny that awaits her child.

Beside her are statues of Cosmas and Damian, patron saints of the Medici, by Montorsoli and Montelupo respectively. The overall mood is like a scene from informal daily life rather than one of rigorous piety, thus demonstrating Michelangelo's ability to rise above his rebellious temperament and attain true freedom of artistic expression.

19. *Interior of the Medici Chapel*, 1520-1534. San Lorenzo, Florence.

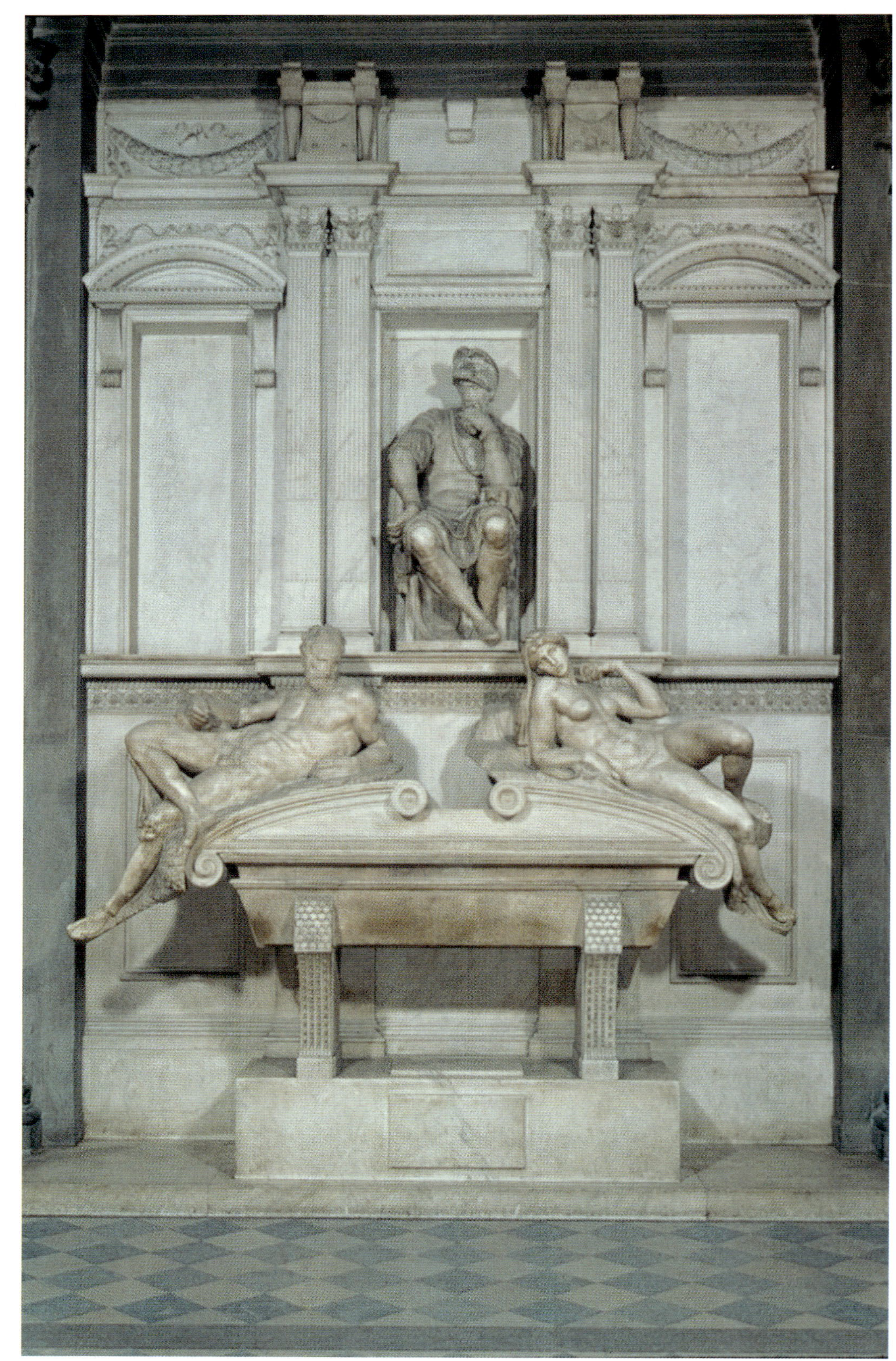

20. *Tomb of Lorenzo de Medici,* 1525-1527. Marble. San Lorenzo, Florence.

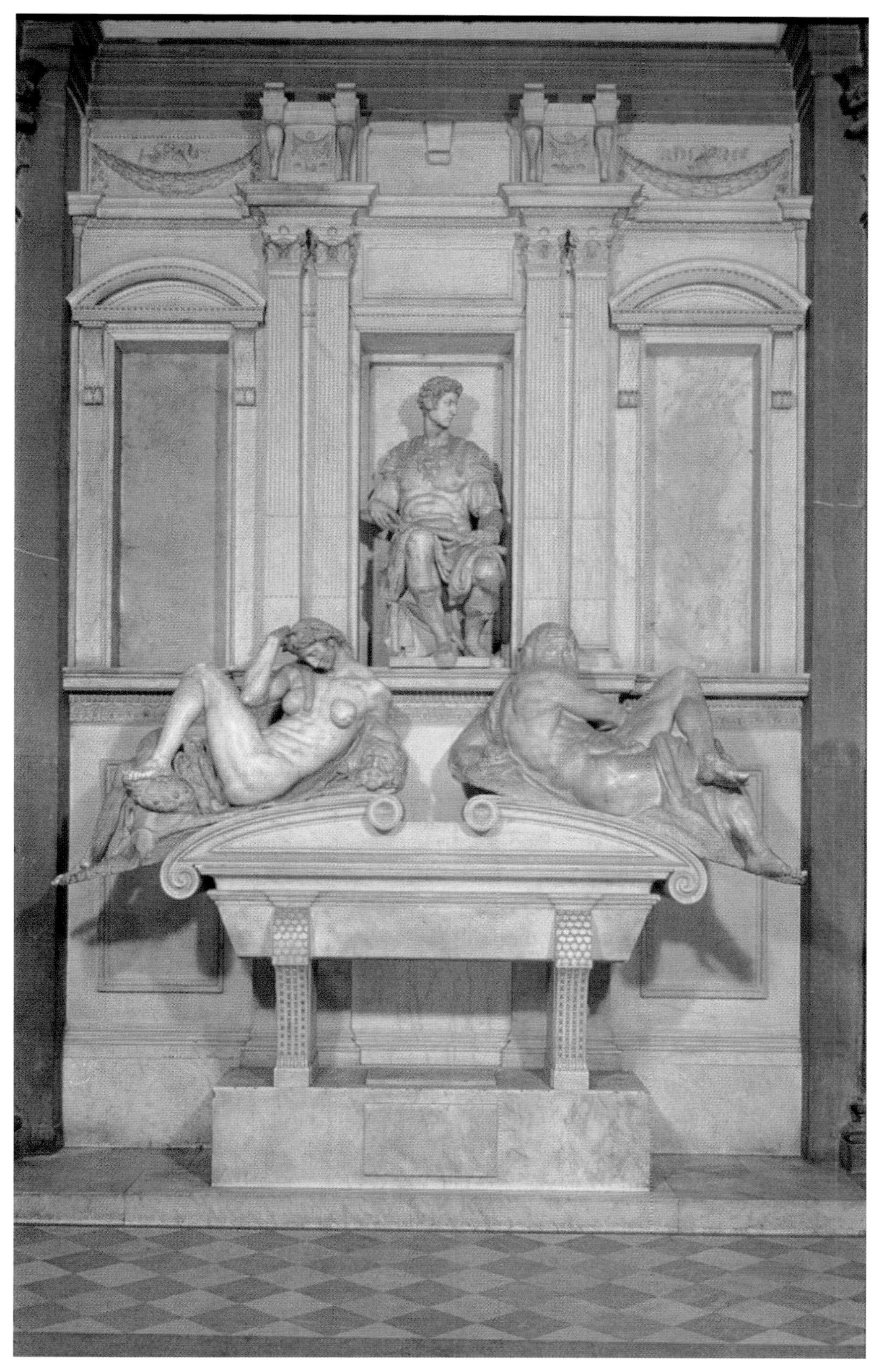

21. *Tomb of Julius de Medici,* 1525-1527. Marble. San Lorenzo, Florence.

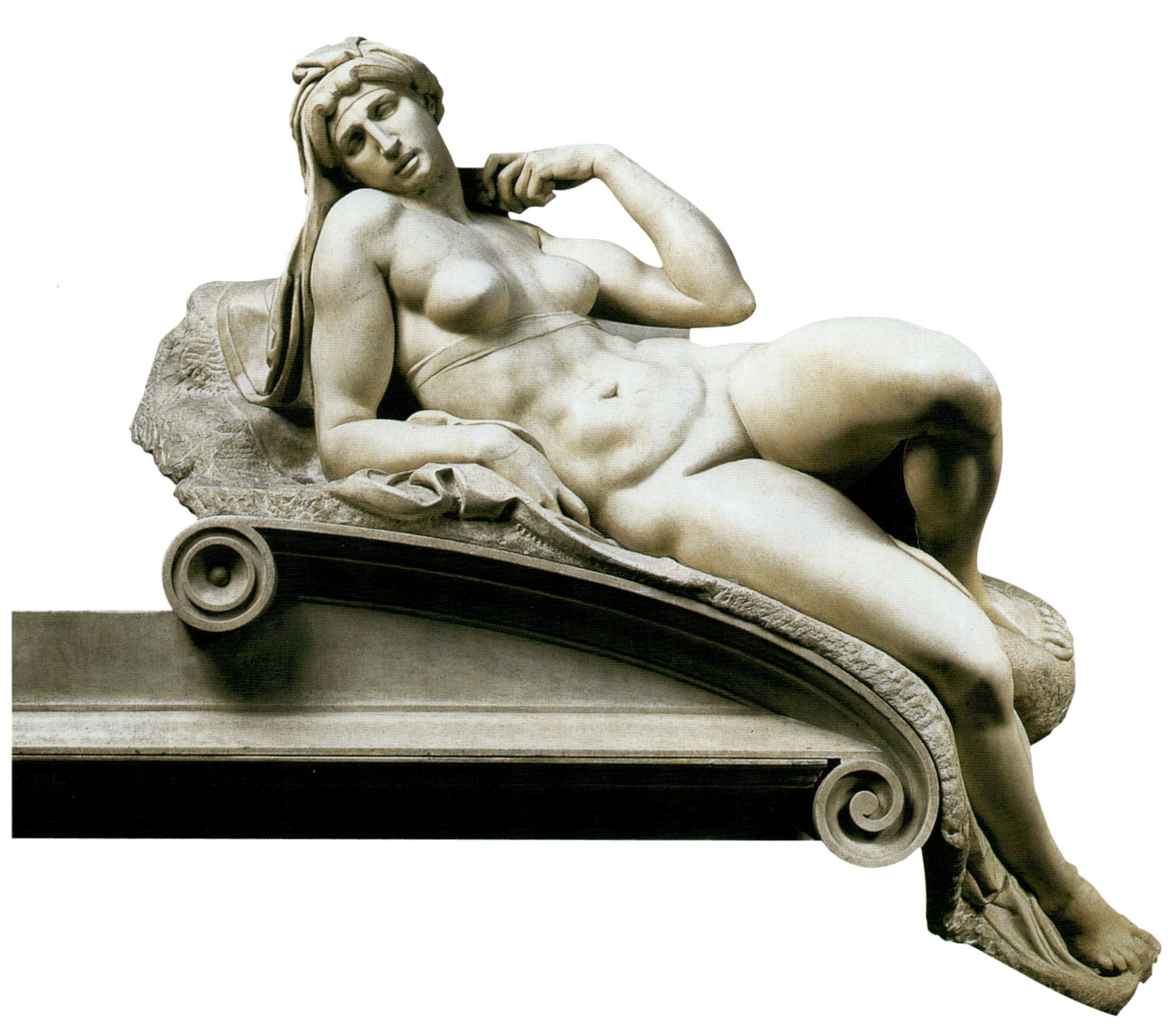

22. *Dawn,* 1525-1527. Detail of the tomb of Lorenzo of Medici. Marble. Medici Chapel, San Lorenzo, Florence.

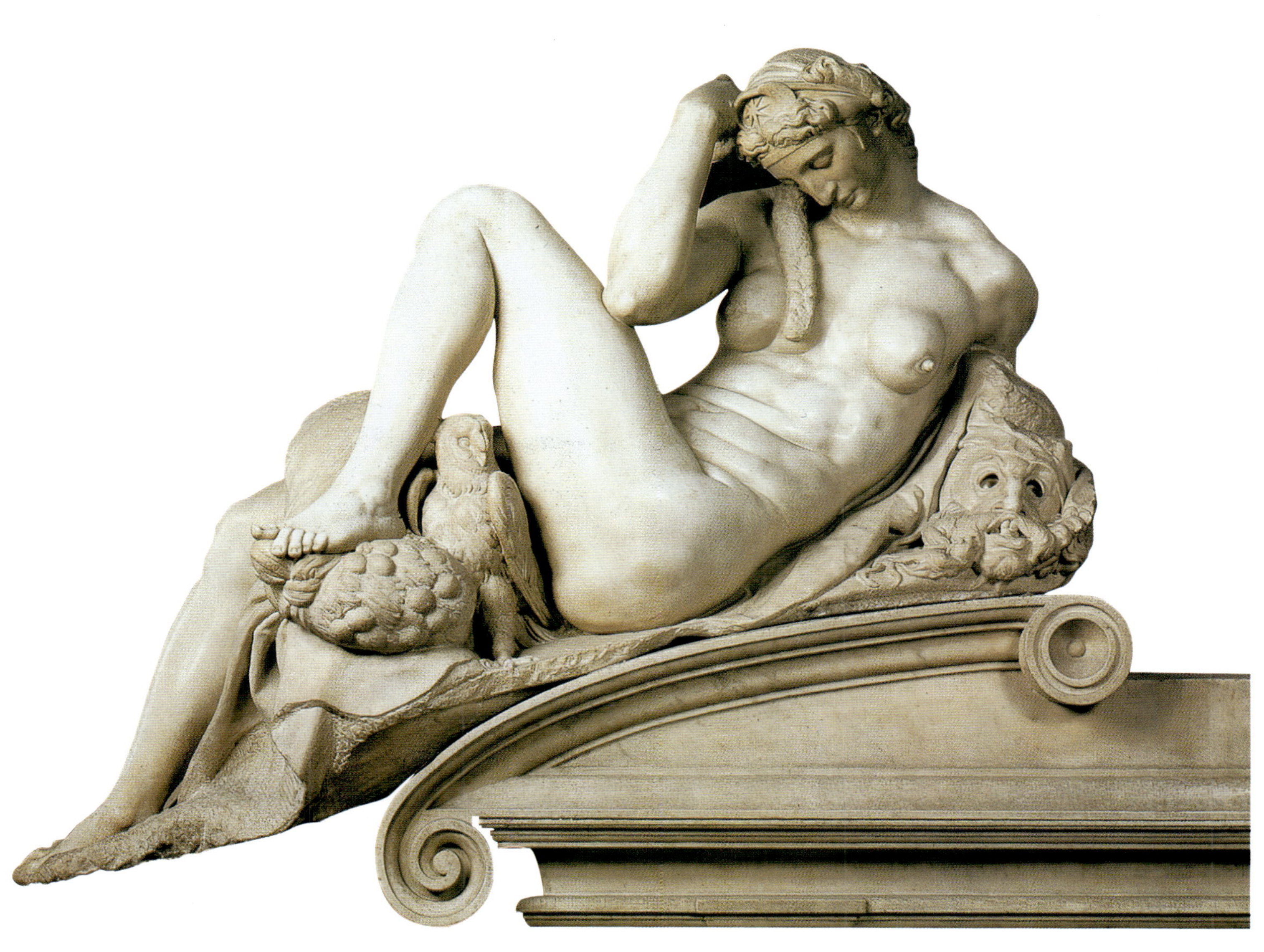

23. *Night,* 1525-1527. Detail of the tomb of Julius de Medici. Marble, 194 cm long. Medici Chapel, San Lorenzo, Florence.

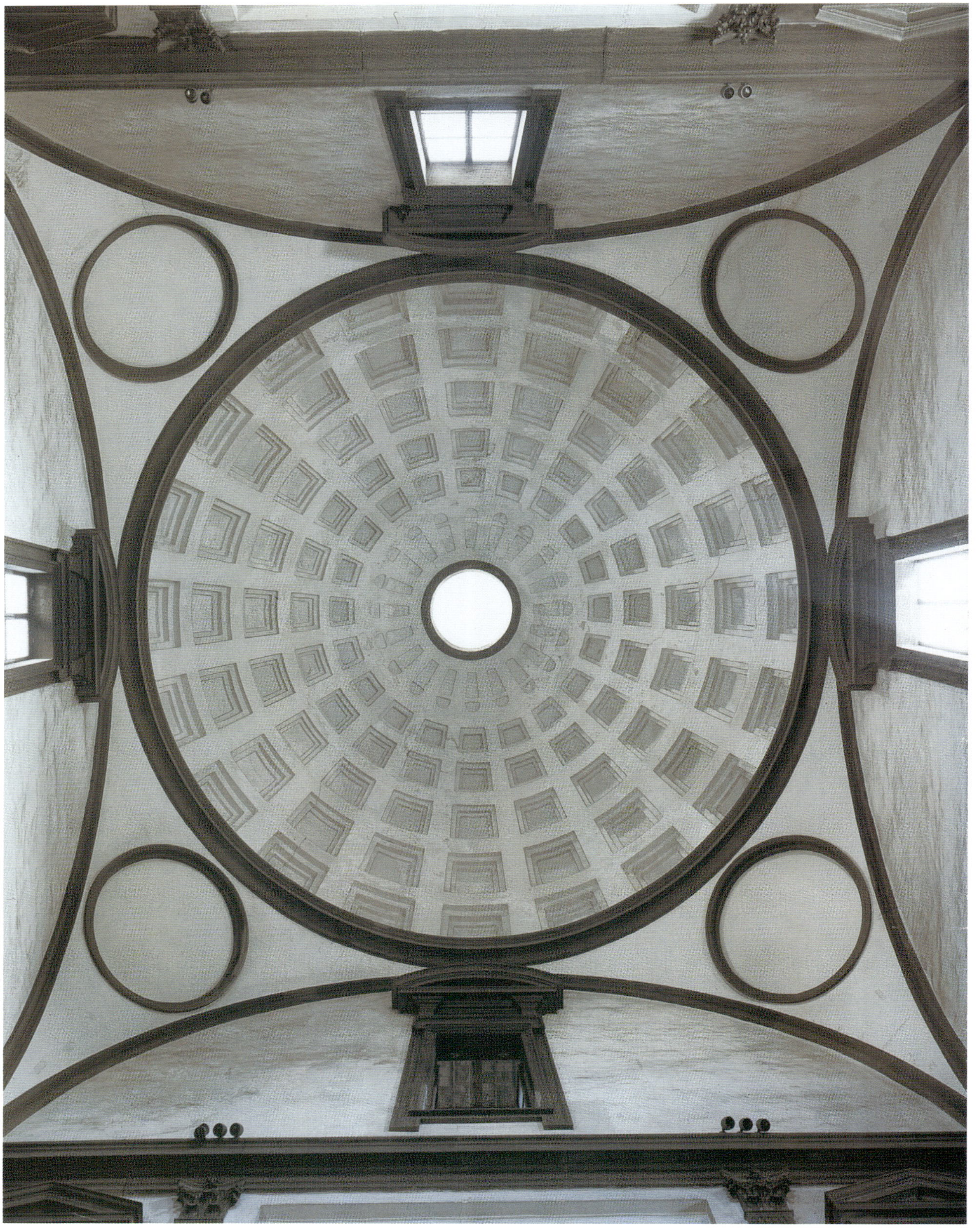

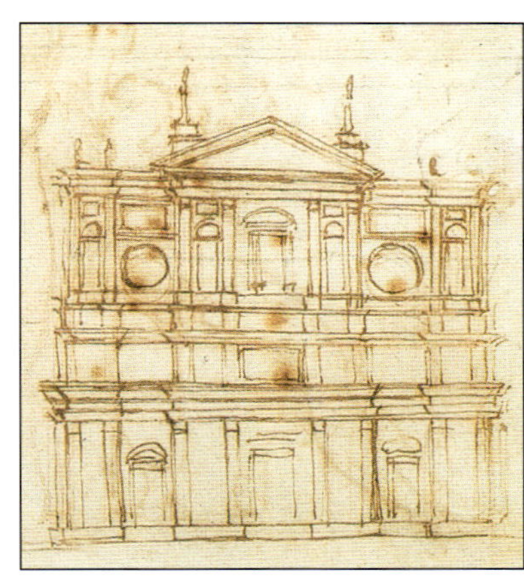

The Architect

Michelangelo entered architecture fairly late in life as his focus turned to the relationship between a work and the space it occupies. Renaissance values were already trying to fit the size of architectural elements to the dimensions of the human body. For his part, Michelangelo felt that proportions were only one consideration; he argued that the viability and functionality of a building were subsidiary although essential elements.

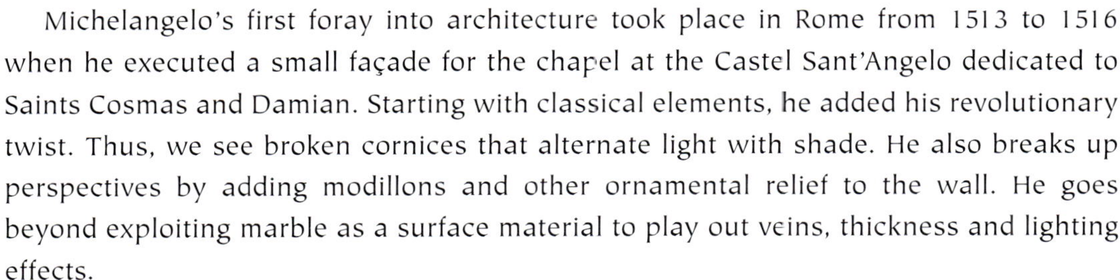

Michelangelo's first foray into architecture took place in Rome from 1513 to 1516 when he executed a small façade for the chapel at the Castel Sant'Angelo dedicated to Saints Cosmas and Damian. Starting with classical elements, he added his revolutionary twist. Thus, we see broken cornices that alternate light with shade. He also breaks up perspectives by adding modillons and other ornamental relief to the wall. He goes beyond exploiting marble as a surface material to play out veins, thickness and lighting effects.

The following year, he went on to do the windows of the Medici Palace in Florence. There, Michelangelo's first major architectural work was the façade of the San Lorenzo Chapel in 1519. Though never finished, it combines all three of the artist's main skill and demonstrates his flair for contrasting lines, colours and lighting effects.

During the same stay, Michelangelo won the commission for what became the Laurentian Library after Pope Clement VII bequeathed his book collection to the Medici to the San Lorenzo Church. The original agreement was for a reading room for manuscript research. The most remarkable element of the building is easily the entrance adjoining the church, with a splendid vestibule and tripartite stairway leading down to the reading room.

In 1523, Antonio da Sangallo began work on a façade and inner courtyard for the Farnese Palace, one of Rome's most beautiful structures. In 1534, Alessandro Farnese became Pope Paul III. His new position induced him to order a bigger façade and a more spacious courtyard. Michelangelo was asked to do the cornice in addition to supervising the entire worksite after Sangallo's death in 1546. In only two years at the palace, Michelangelo left his indelible mark on it by redesigning it entirely.

24. Interior view of the dome of the Medici Chapel, San Lorenzo.

25. Drawing of *The Facade of the Church of San Lorenzo*, 1517. Quill, red and black stone, 21.2 x 14.4 cm. Casa Buonarroti, Florence.

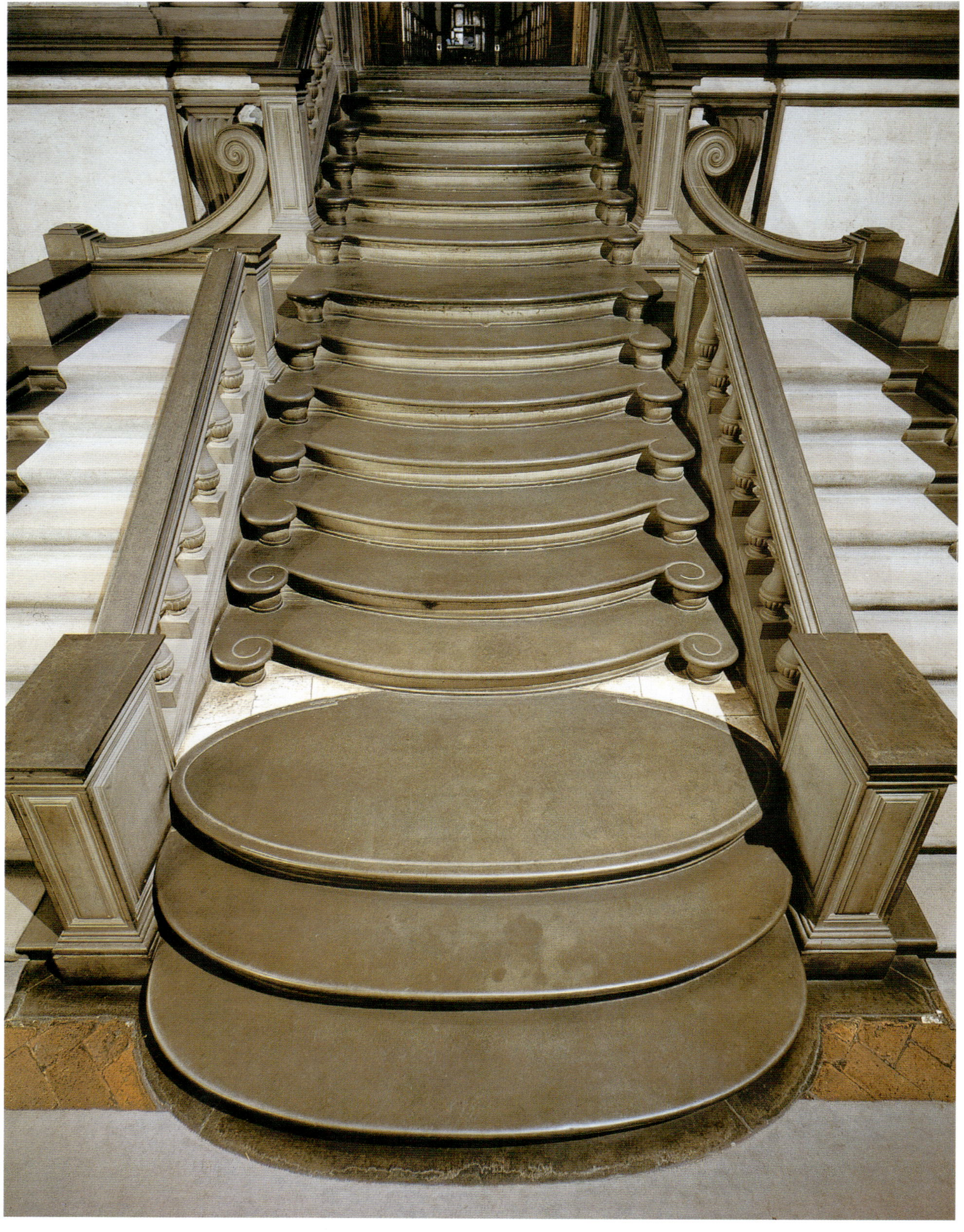

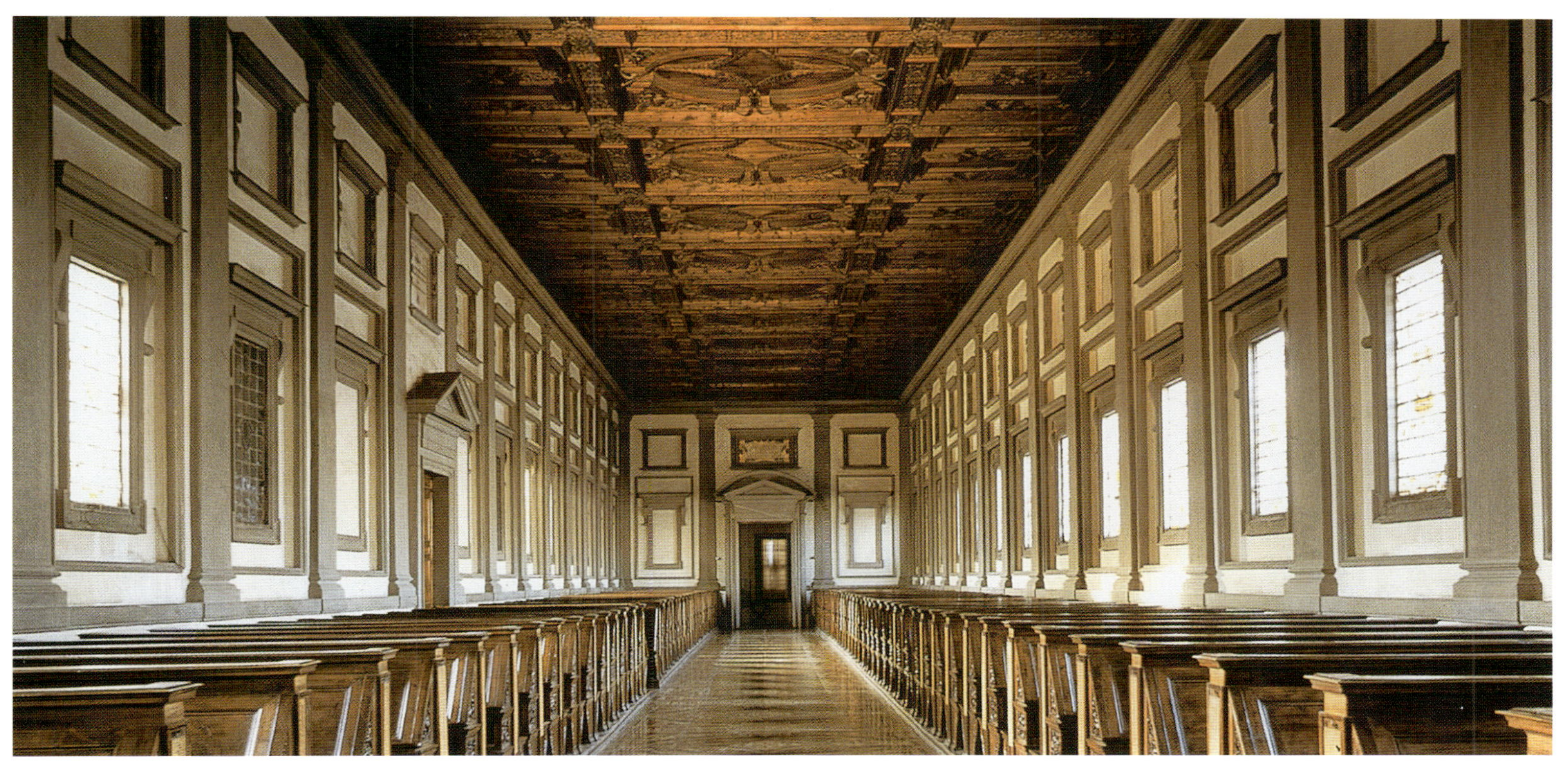

He turned the visual proportions upside down by moving the heavier elements high up and supporting them with a mix of arches and openings where he played off solid volumes against voids. Succombing to pressure from leading Romans and Humanists in 1538, Paul III called in Michelangelo to remodel the buildings surrounding the Campidoglio (Capitol) to achieve greater overall harmony. The artist envisioned a vast project that blended both classical and contemporary perfection. For what remained the civic and political heart of the city, he laid out an *ovoid* form centred on a statue he disliked of Emperor Marcus Aurelius.

Then he drafted new facades for the towering Palazzo dei Conservatori and Palazzo dei Senatore on the Campidoglio with a view to creating greater aesthetic coherence while preserving their monumental character. He went on to drawings that would give the Capitoline dramatic magnificence equal to that of the Palazzo dei Conservatori, opposite where it was to be built. Michelangelo saw these three visually coherent constructions as an ideal way of highlighting the summit of the Capitoline Hill. For the paving, he wanted an outwardly radiating display of grey and white stones that upset the existing set of proportions.

26. *Staircase of the Vestibule.*
Laurentine Library,
San Lorenzo, Florence.

27. *Reading room of the Laurentine Library,*
San Lorenzo, Florence.

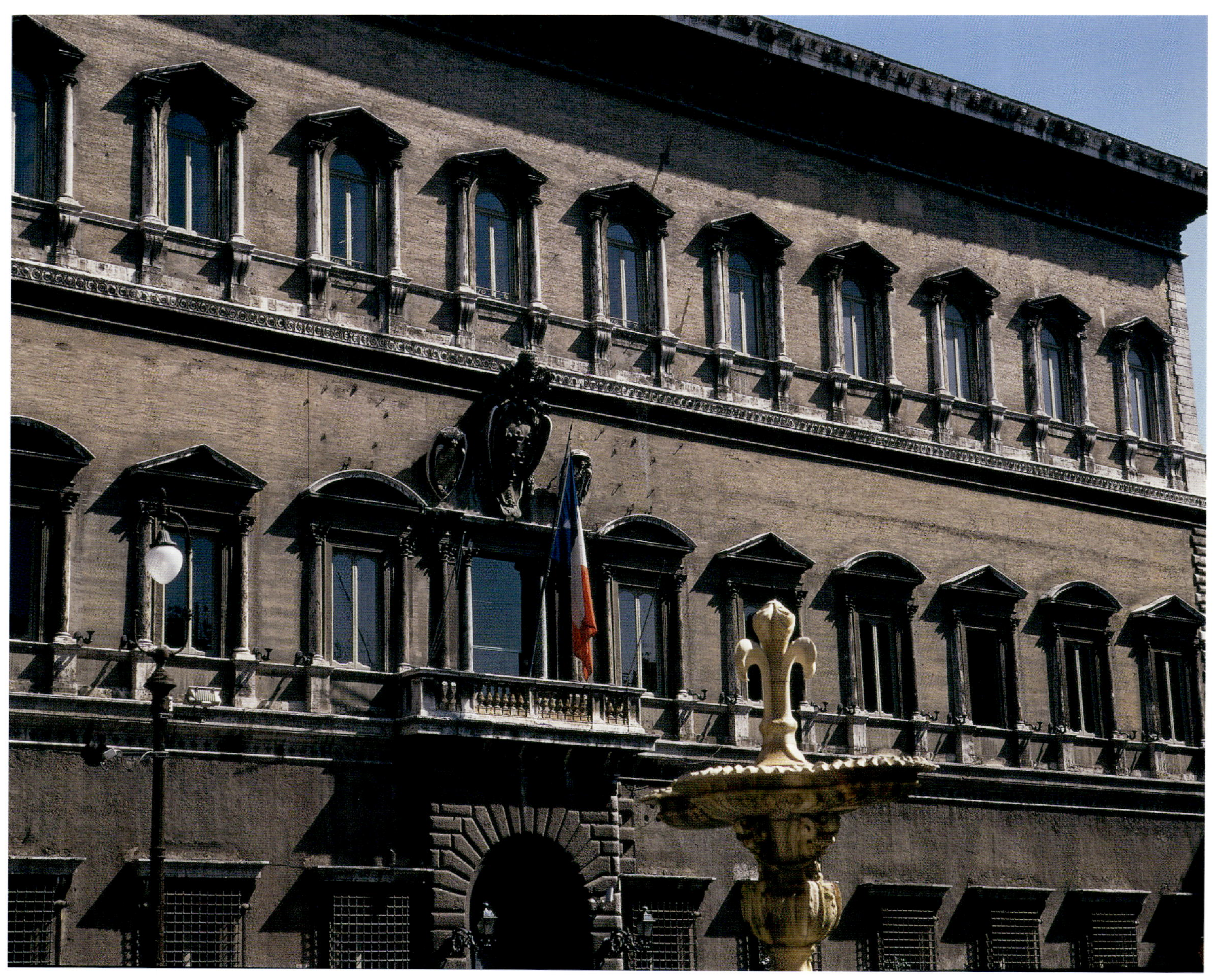

28. *Palazzo Farnese,* Rome. View of the façade, design begun by Antonio da Sangallo the Younger and continued by Michelangelo, Giacoma Vignola and Giacomo della Porta. 1517-1589.

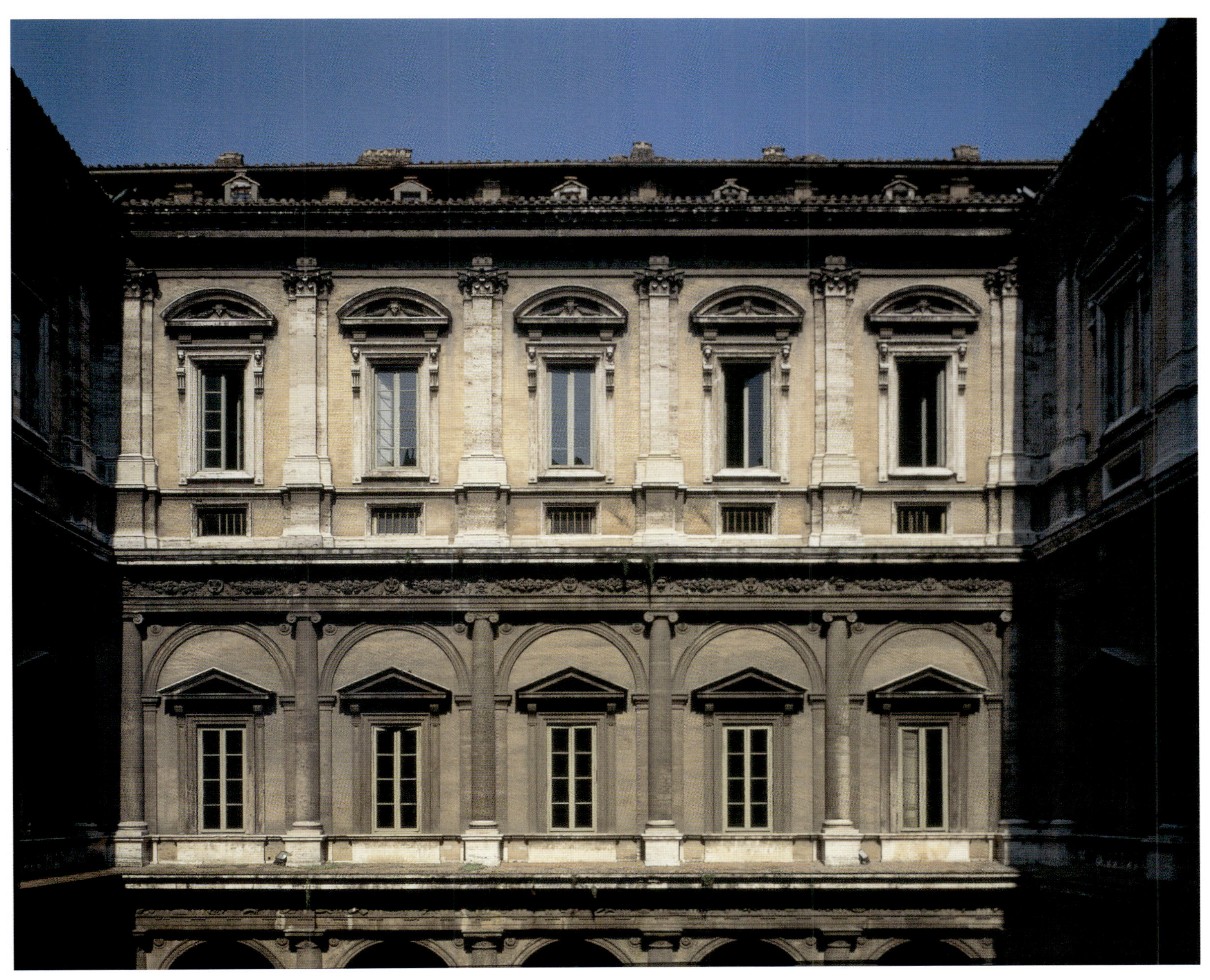

29. *Palazzo Farnese,* Rome. The facade of the inner courtyard, detail of the second storey designed by Antonio da Sangallo the Younger in 1517 and the third by Michelangelo between 1549-1569.

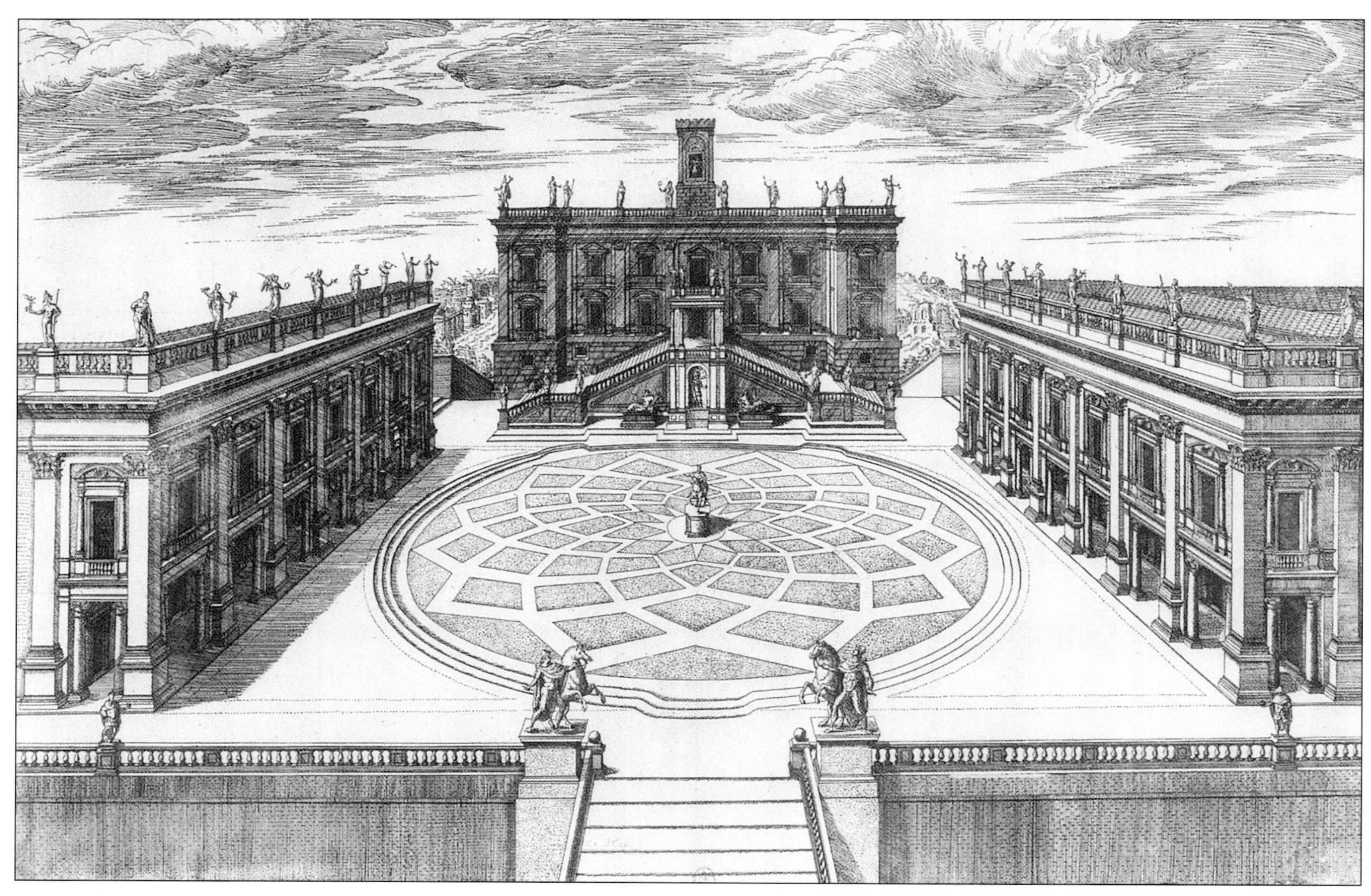

30. Etienne Dupérac, *Michelangelo's project for the Capitole,* 1558. Carving. Bibliotèque Nationale, Paris.

31. *View of today's Capitole,* Rome.

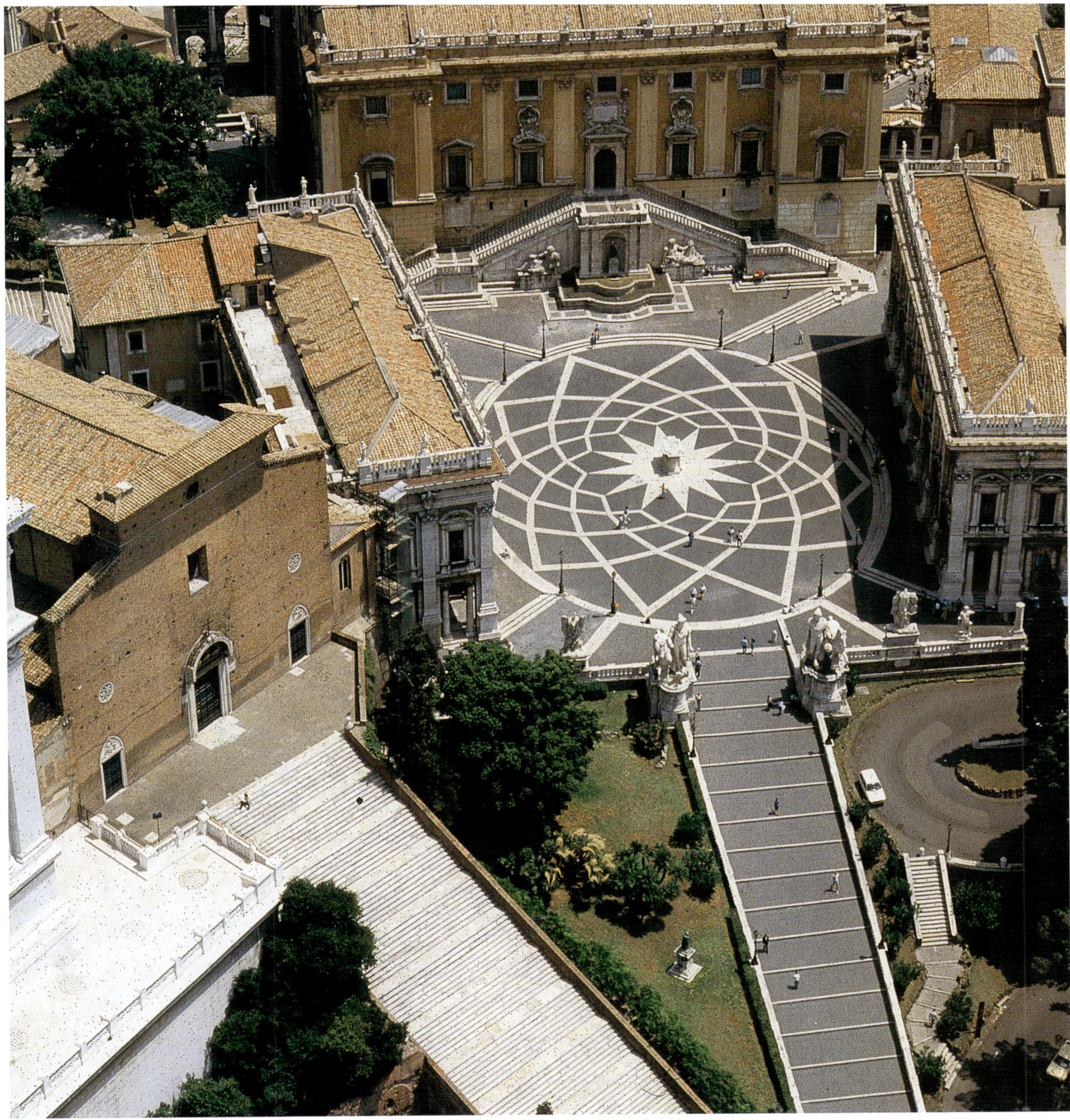

Going further, he added in a large majestic stair leading into the sloping, trapezoidal piazza. But the entire work would only become a reality in the 17th century – except for the paving, finally ordered and completed to Michelangelo's specifications by Benito Mussolini in 1940.

Michelangelo devoted all the energy of his final years to rebuilding St. Peter's Cathedral in Rome, thus following in the footsteps of artists such as Raphael, Baldassari, Peruzzi, Sangallo and Bramante. Starting out from a Greek cross, Michelangelo injected movement into the edifice in order to reduce its monumental weight. Straying far afield from Bramante's vision of a pantheonesque design, Michelangelo's dome is majestic with a twist of Florentine influence.

Rising 136.5 metres into the sky, the dome has a strong upward thrust from the lines that rise along its surface finally converging on the stately drum at the base of the bell tower. At the time of Michelangelo's death, construction was far enough advanced for him to reasonably expect execution without modifications. Moreover, his friend Vasari had to the foresight to coax a wooden scale model from the master that would become crucial to faithful completion.

Michelangelo's last completed works were the Santa Maria degli Angeli Church and Porta Pia, both commissioned in 1561 by Pope Pius IV. After careers in sculpture, painting, army engineering and architecture, at the age of 85, the master could henceforth call himself an urban planner. The Porta Via still stands as a fine example of Michelangelo's penchant for architecture on a colossal scale.

Michelangelo's longevity was rare for his time and in 1561 he was still chiseling away, enhancing the beauty of the Eternal City after all the other great masters of the Renaissance lay long buried. When Pope Pius IV handed over the Baths of Diocletian to the Carthusian Order to construct a church and cloister, Michelangelo transformed them into the church of Santa Maria degli Angeli.

32. *St. Peter's,* viewed from the West, 1546-1564. Vatican.

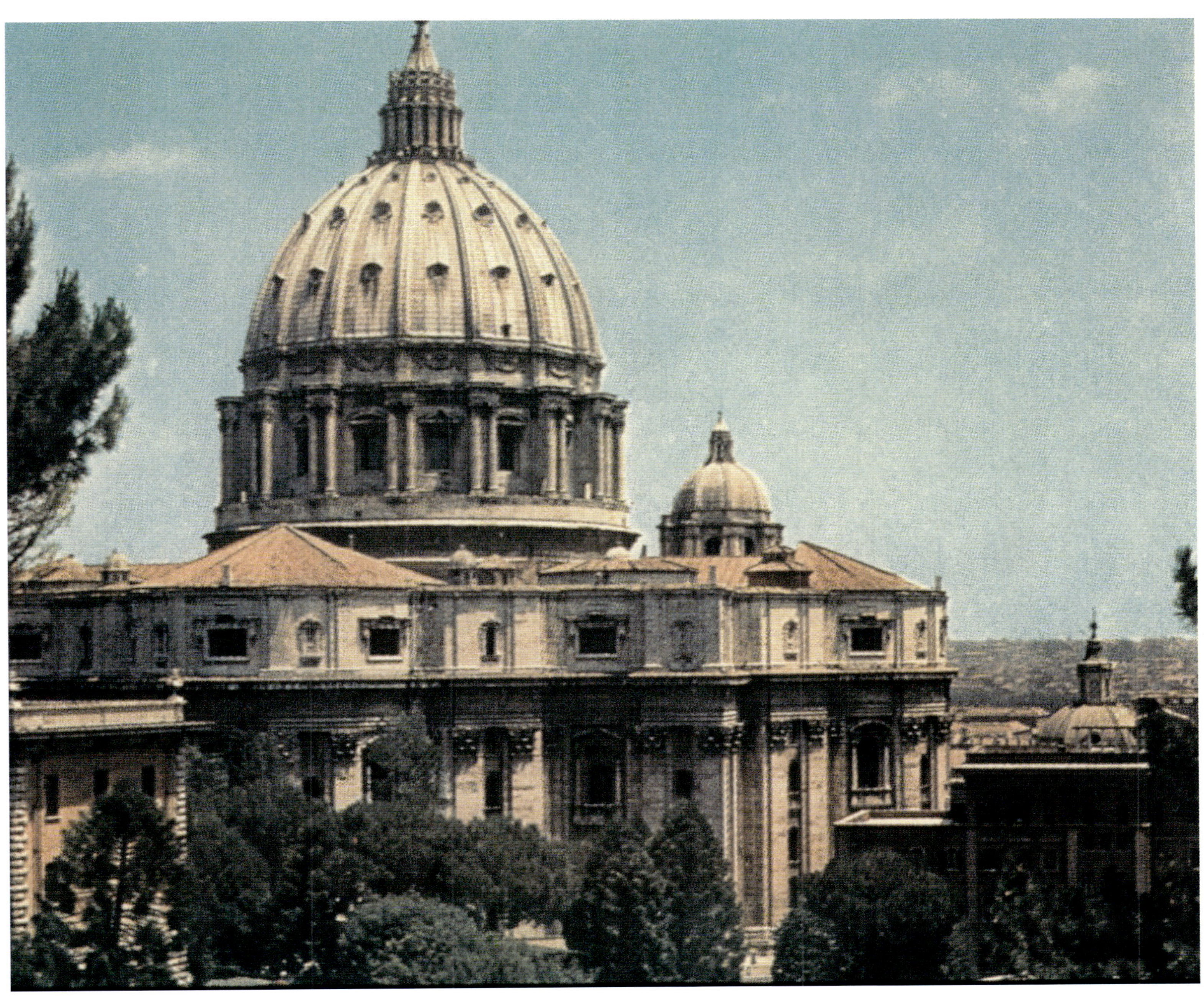

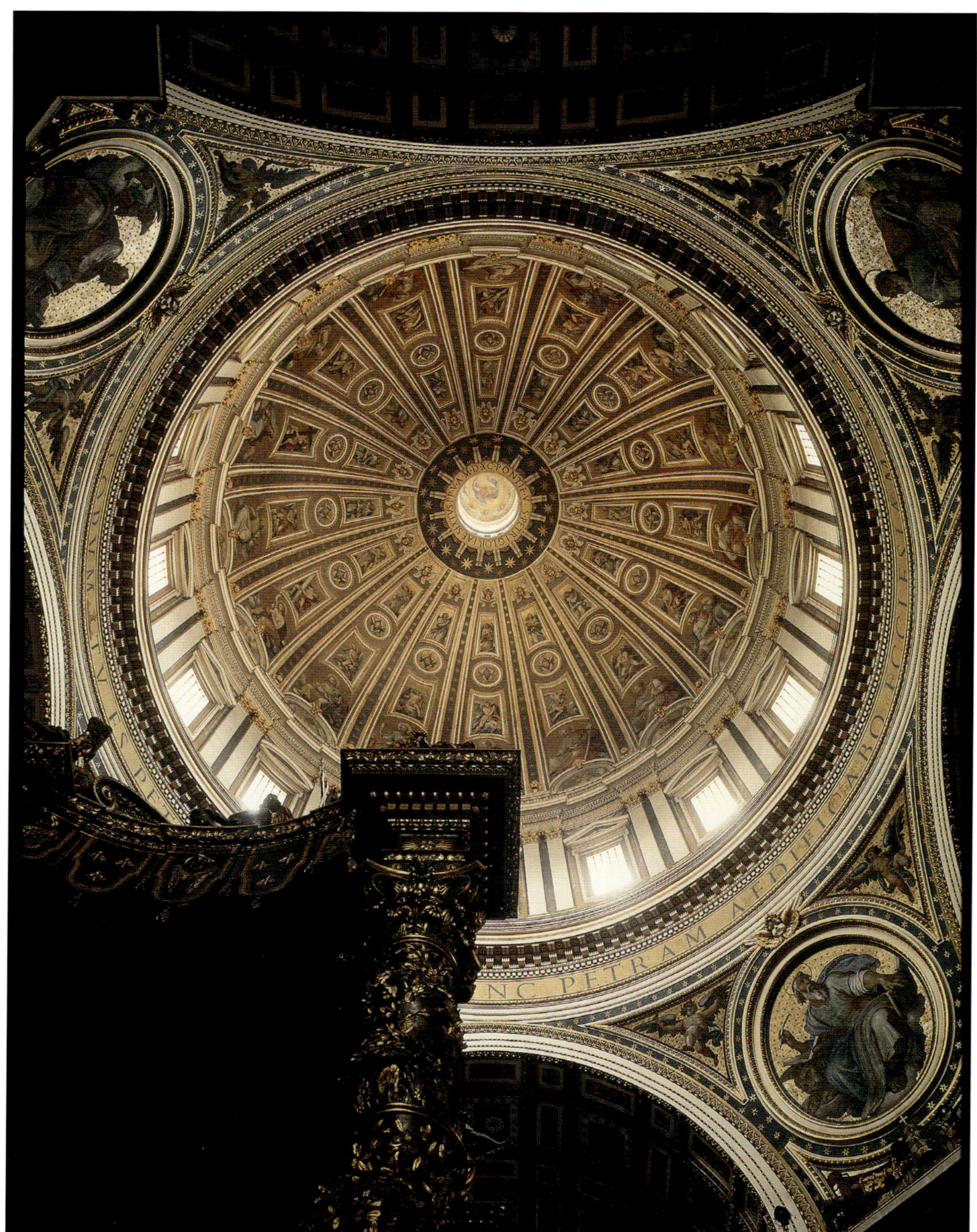

33. *View of the interior of the Dome*, begun by Michelangelo in 1546 and completed by Domenico Fontana in 1593. St. Peter's, Vatican.

34. *Aerial view of the Basilic of Saint Peter.* Picture by Giacomo Della Porta.

35. *Porta Pia*, 1561. Rome.

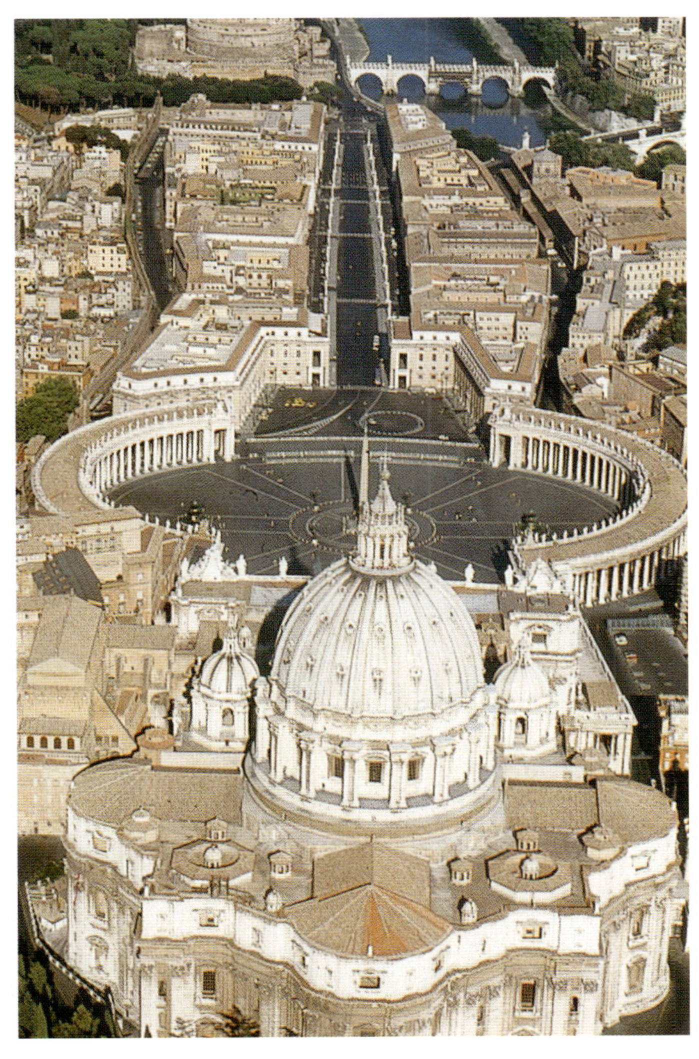

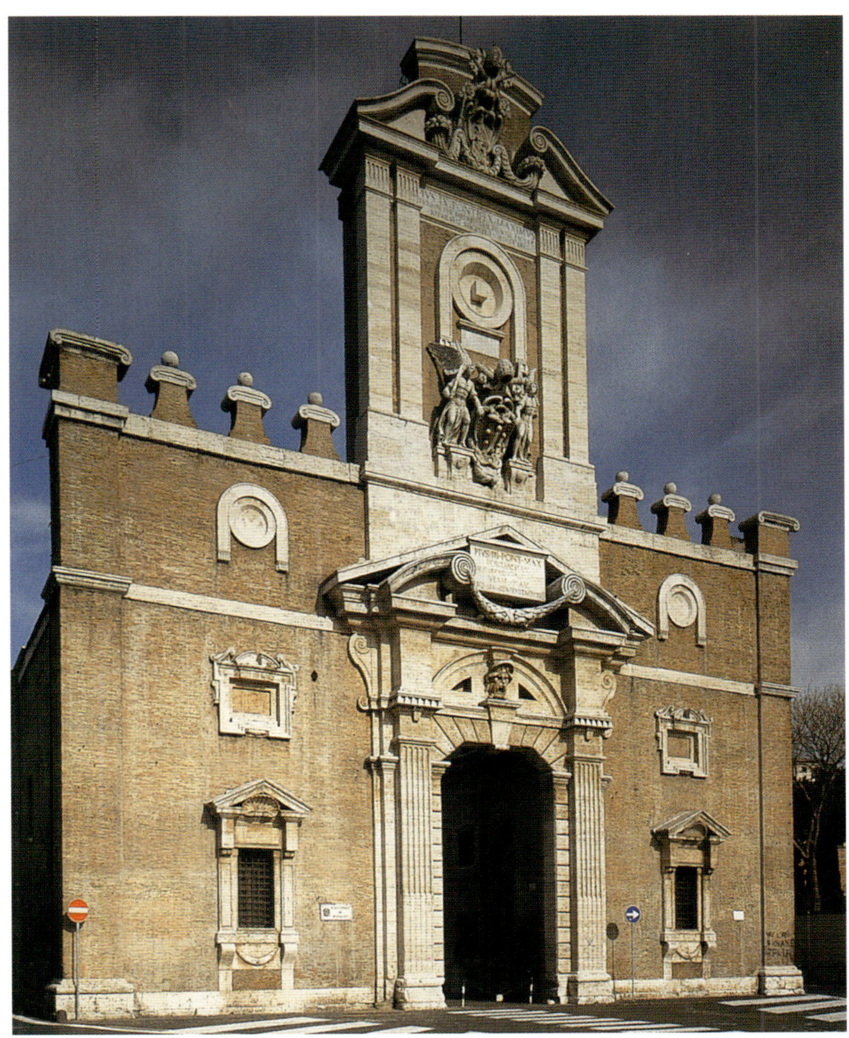

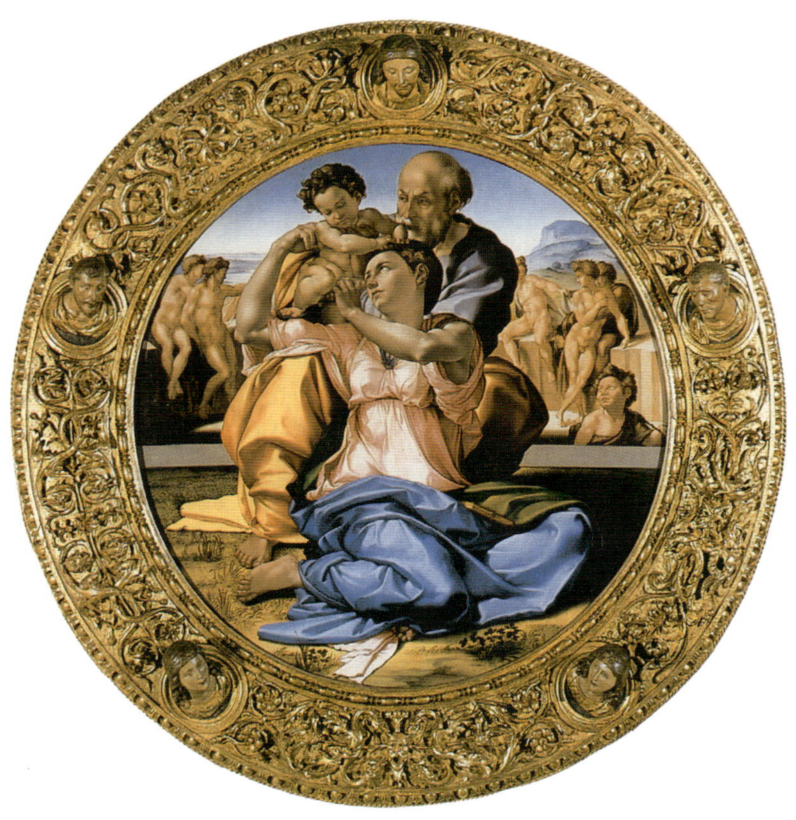

Beyond Peerless Painting

36. *Tondo Doni*, circa 1504. Circular wooden panel painted with tempera (watered down), diameter of 120cm. The Offices, Florence.

37. *Sistine Chapel,* vault, panel of the *Last Judgement*, north and south sides, after restoration of frescoes, 1508-1541.

Around 1507, Agnolo Doni commissioned Michelangelo for a representation of *Doni Tondo* (*The Holy Family*). Here, Michelangelo builds the composition along a vertical axis, with the three figures bonding and nourishing each other via eye contact and arm gestures: the Da Vinci touch is there, like it or not. This was his first truly complete painting and it shows a confident, extremely personal approach to his subjects with a fine command of the brush.

In 1484, Giovanino de'Dolci finished the Sistine Chapel in the Vatican City under Pope Sixtus IV. Its walls were covered in frescoes by a variety of artists, who had started work in 1481. Their names include masters such as Pinturicchio, Botticelli, Perugi, Ghirlandaio and Signorelli. In 1508, Pope Julius II called Michelangelo in from Florence for the still naked ceiling of the Sistine Chapel. The immenseness of the vault made him reluctant but he relented and completed it in 1512. No further improvements to this enchanting edifice were to be made for the next 23 years.

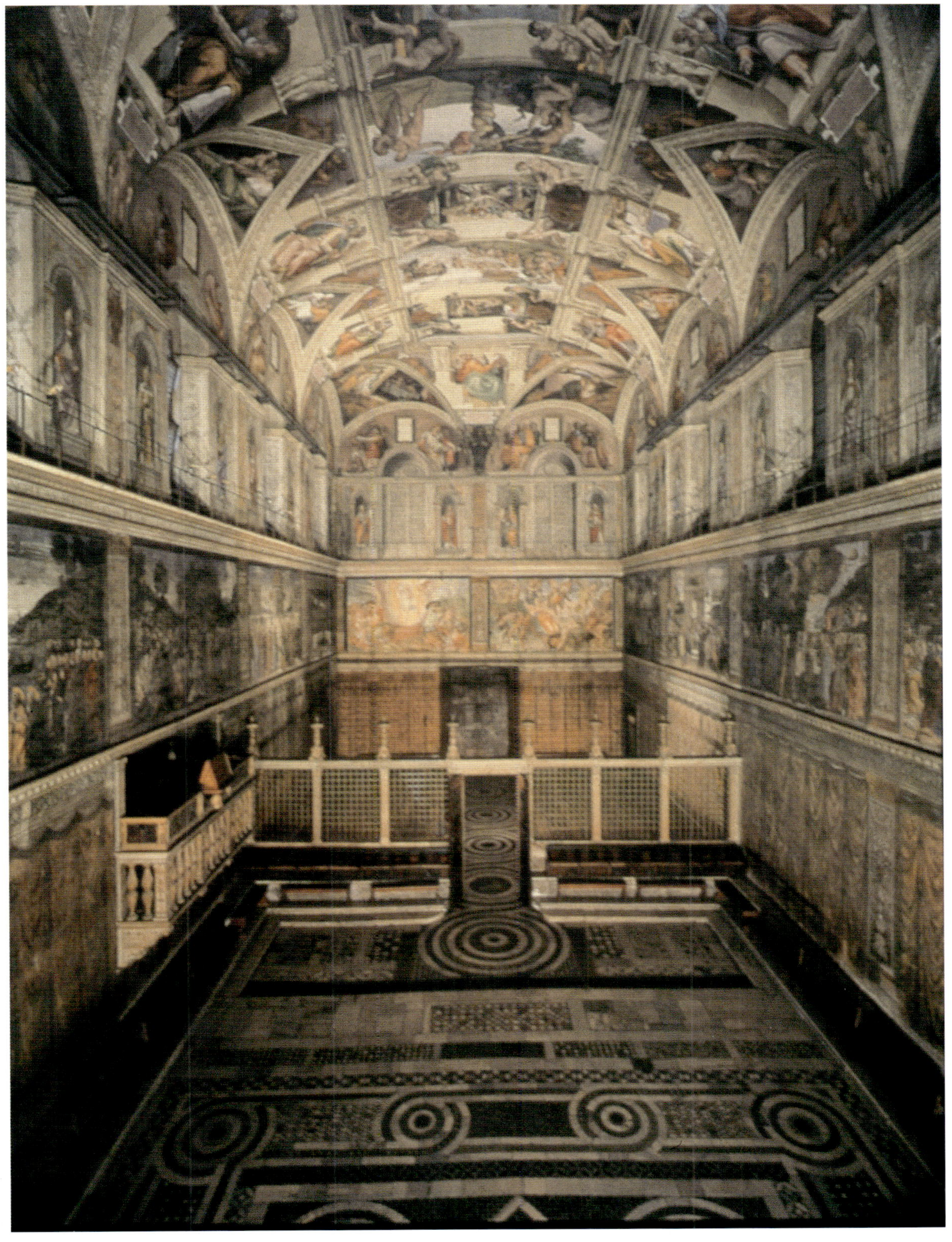

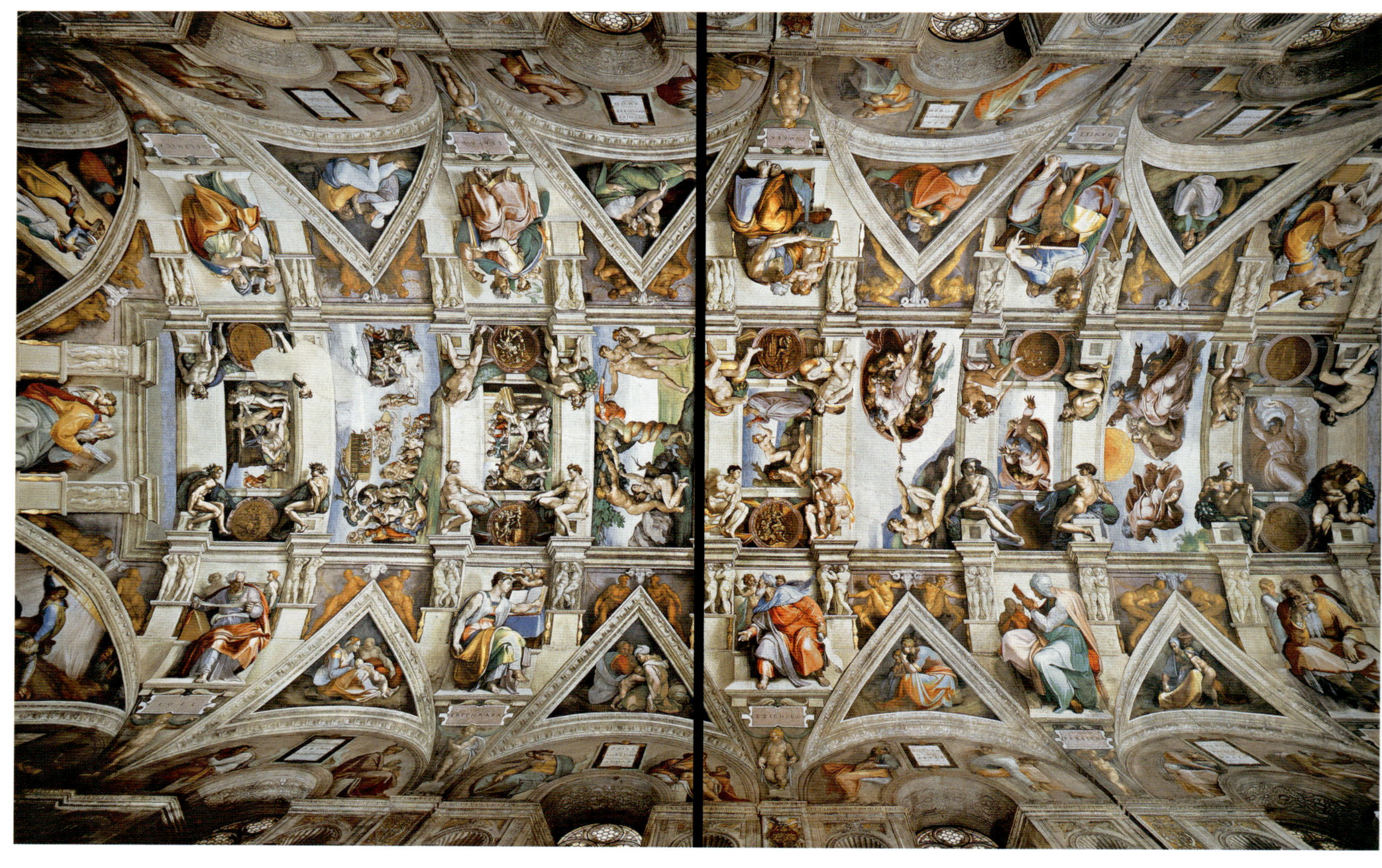

38. *Vault* of the Sistine Chapel after restoration. Vatican.

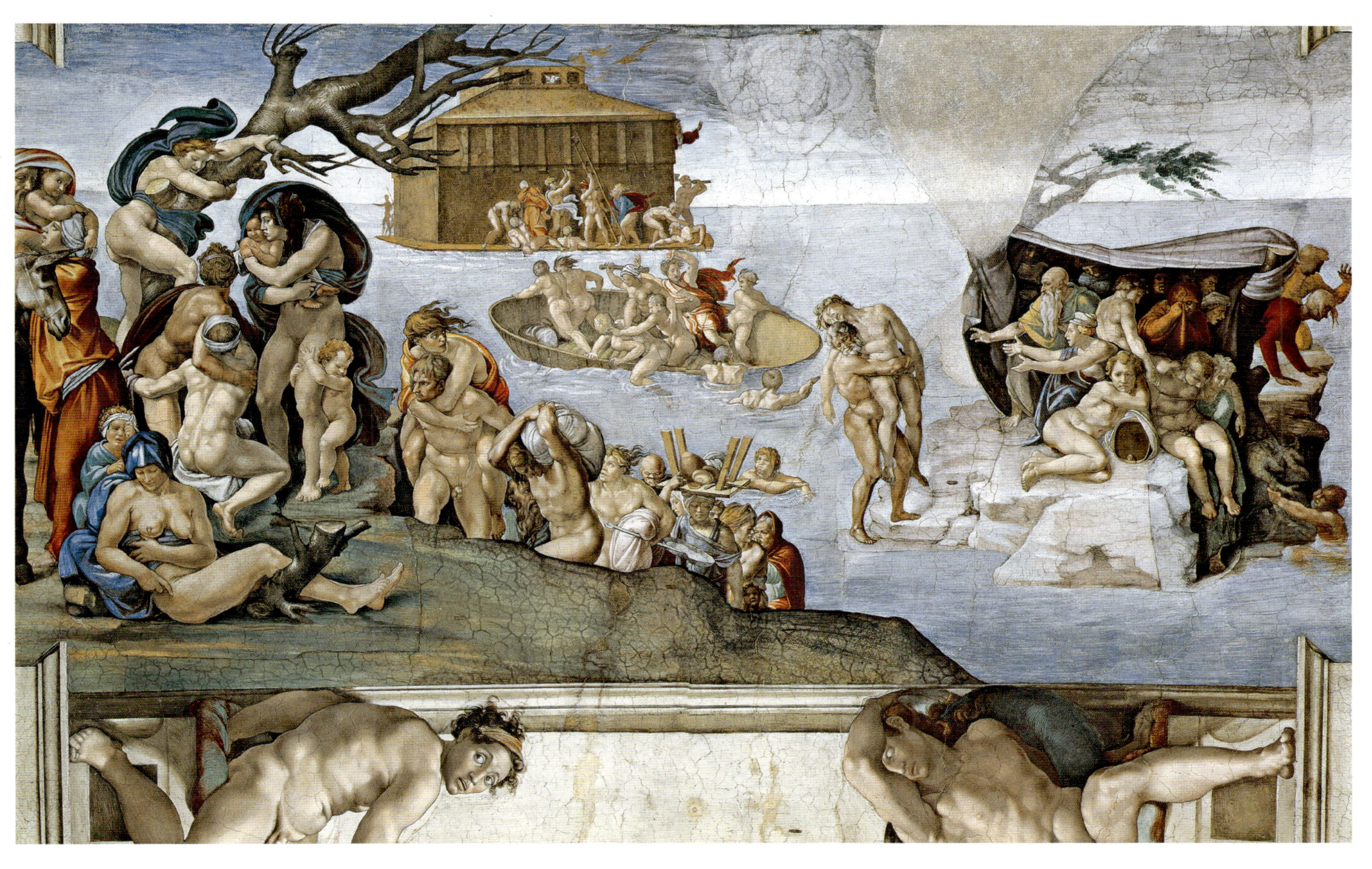

39. *The Deluge* (second panel of the archway). Fresco. Sistine Chapel, Vatican.

Succeeding Clement VII, Pope Paul III invited Michelangelo back to the Sistine Chapel with a commission for the rear wall. It would cost him seven years of hard work. In 1541, his *Last Judgment* was completed and with it, so was the chapel. Quickly attracting both high praise and violent criticism, it depicted genitalia that were subsequently painted over in the name of morality.

After initially considering the twelve apostles as pendentives for the vault, Michelangelo finally opted for something more substantial and chose nine key episodes from the Book of Genesis, trimmed with nudes holding medallions depicting scenes from the Book of Kings. At the base of the architectonic structure, Michelangelo seated twelve soothsayers (the prophets and sibyls) on monumental thrones just above the ancestors of Christ, slotted into the arch moldings and lunettes. In each of the four corners is a pendentive showing episodes of the salvation of the Israelites.

Dated around 1535-1541, the *Last Judgment* measures 13.7 m x 12.2 m and contains almost 400 figures who walk, fight, rise skyward, plummet hellward or howl in pain. This commission from Paul III came precisely as Michelangelo was experiencing extreme inner tension over the issues of salvation and life after death; the fresco radiates that torment intensely.

The theme of the *Last Judgment* is the tragedy of a world of sinners whom God must save, in search of salvation while countless human generations rise up from the dust to face their Maker. For Michelangelo, man is unfit to judge: there is neither good nor evil. Only man's innate vulnerability is real, and vice has ever been part of the human equation as it will be on Judgment Day. The artist paints himself into the fresco as the monk pointing to Christ easing himself down upon the clouds.

40. *The Creation of Adam* (sixth panel of the vault), 1508-1512. Fresco. Sistine Chapel, Vatican.

41. *Original Sin* (fourth panel of the vault) Fresco. Sistine Chapel, Vatican.

Vasari recalled the "stupor and admiration" of the public when the scaffolding was withdrawn and Pope Paul III arrived to attend vespers on October 31 1541. Indeed, Michelangelo had injected the *Last Judgment* with all his faith, fears and doubts. He cast himself as the observer, watching humanity head for hell with the knowledge that pain is the path to redemption, for he himself painted till it hurt.

Paul III commissioned *The Conversion of St. Paul* and *The Martyrdom of St. Peter*, two frescoes for positioning face-to-face in the Vatican's Pauline Chapel. Work on the first ran from 1542 to 1545 and the second was completed in 1550.

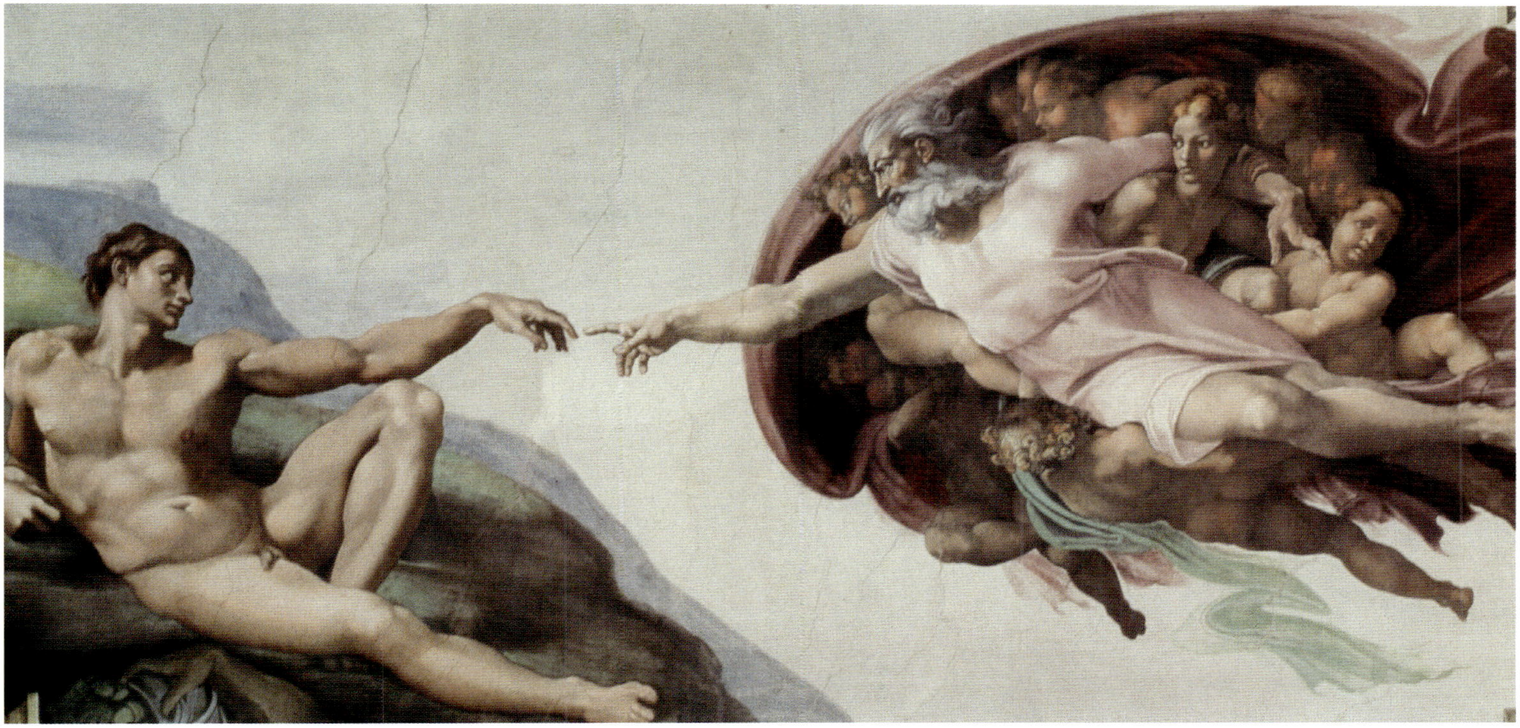

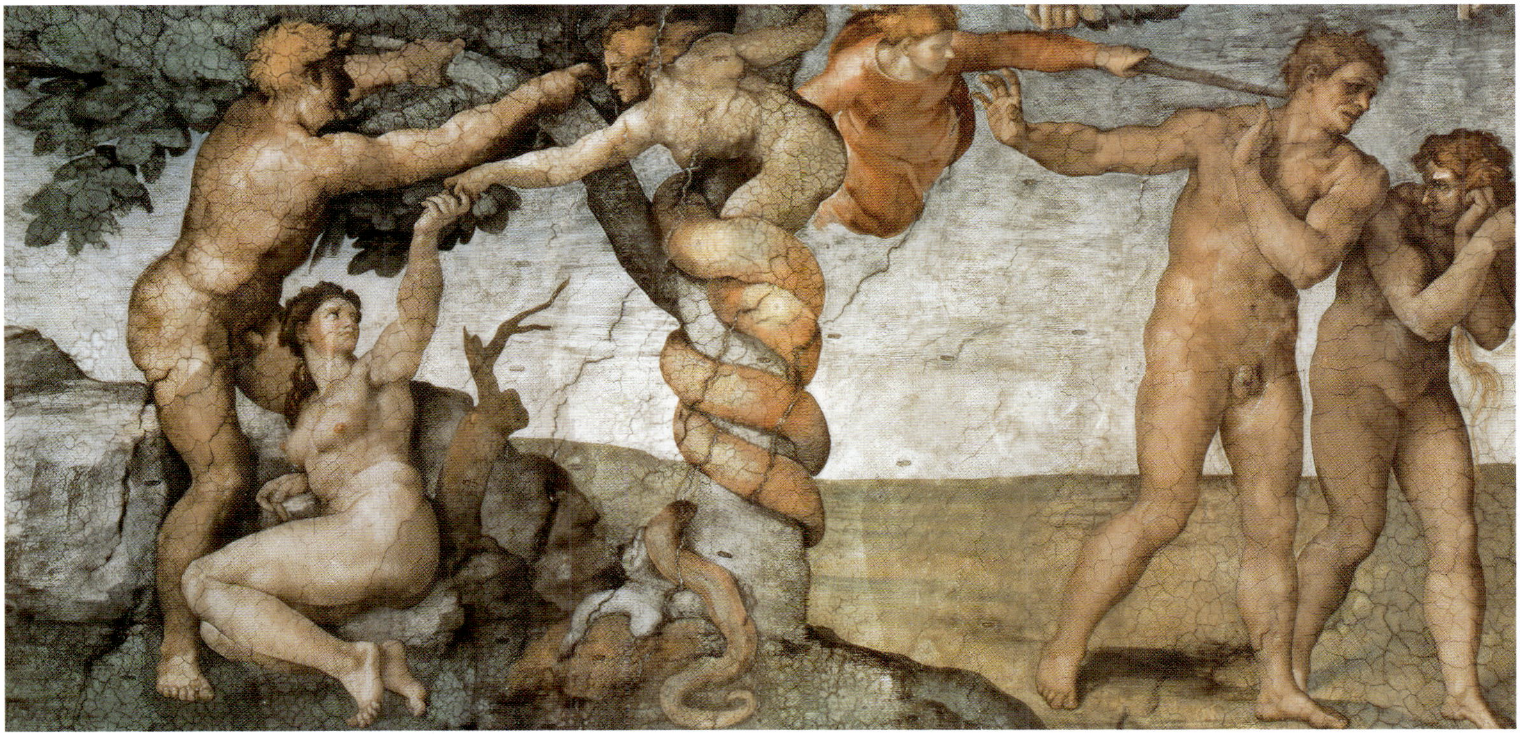

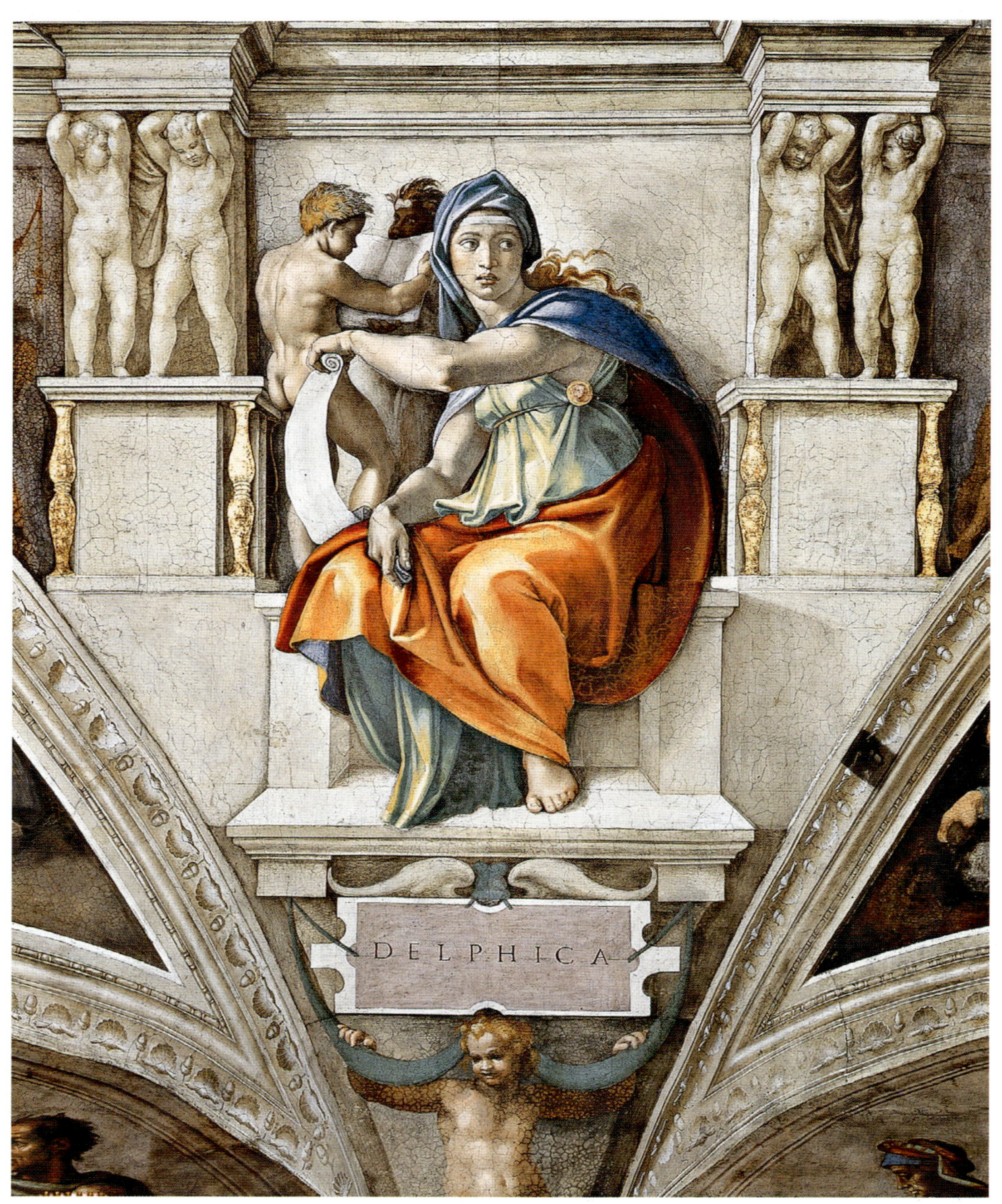

42. *The Delphic Sibyl* (Lateral paintings of the Prophets). Fresco. Sistine Chapel, Vatican.

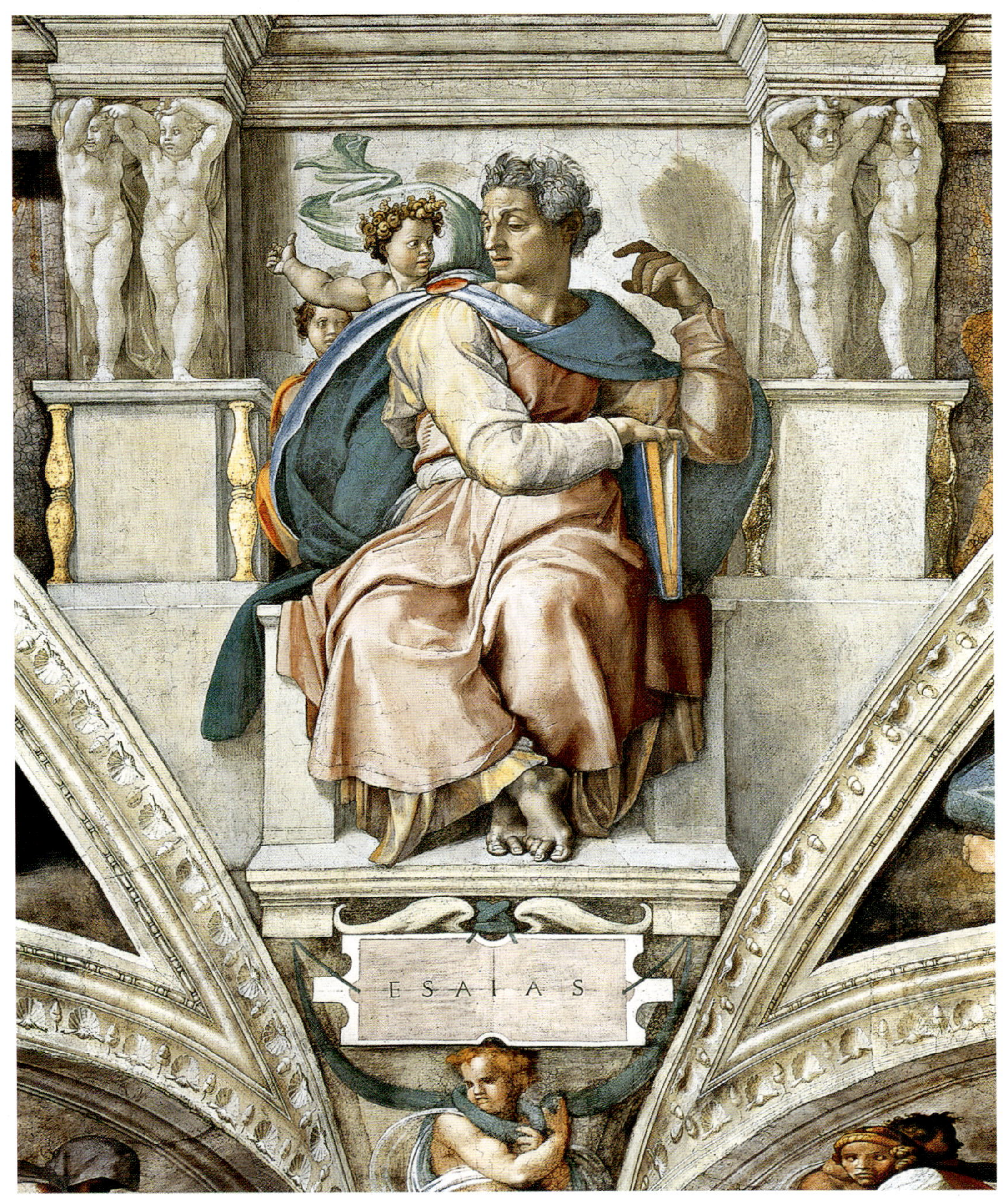

43. *The Prophet Isaiah* (Lateral paintings of the Prophets). Fresco. Sistine Chapel, Vatican.

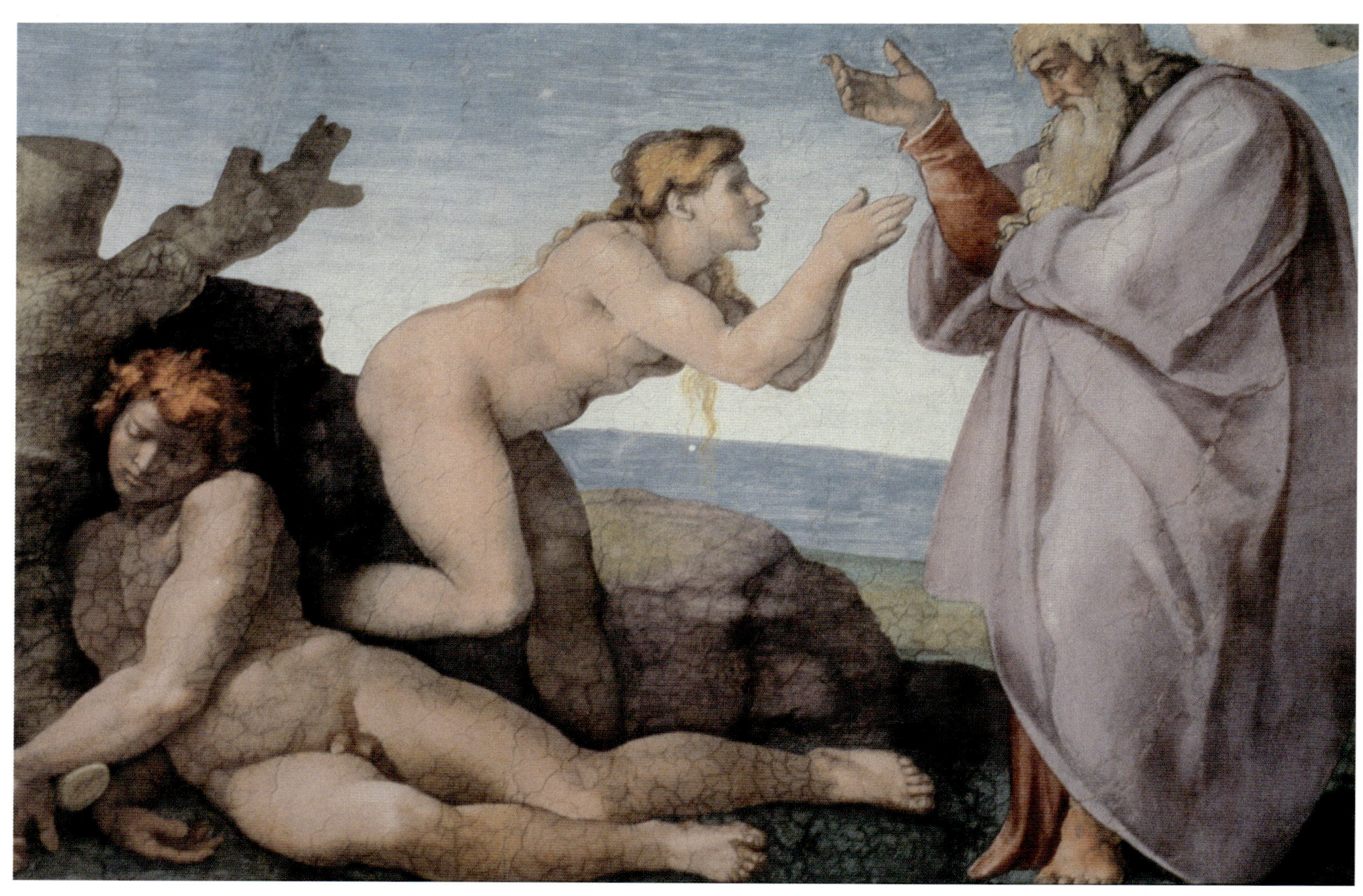

44. *The Creation of Eve* (fifth panel of the vault), 1510-1511. Fresco. Sistine Chapel, Vatican.

45. *The Prophet Ezekiel* (Lateral paintings of the Prophets), 1511. Fresco. Sistine Chapel, Vatican.

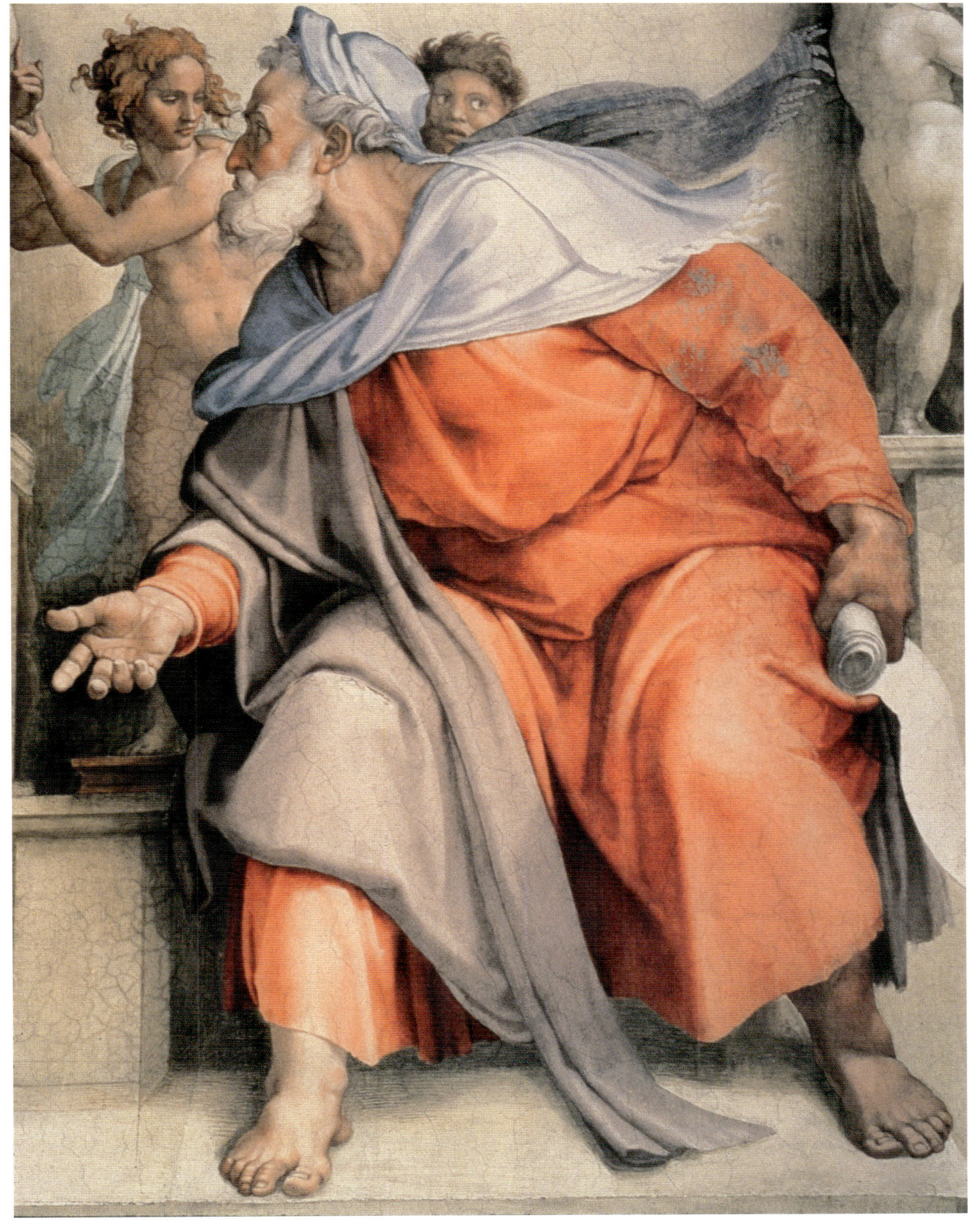

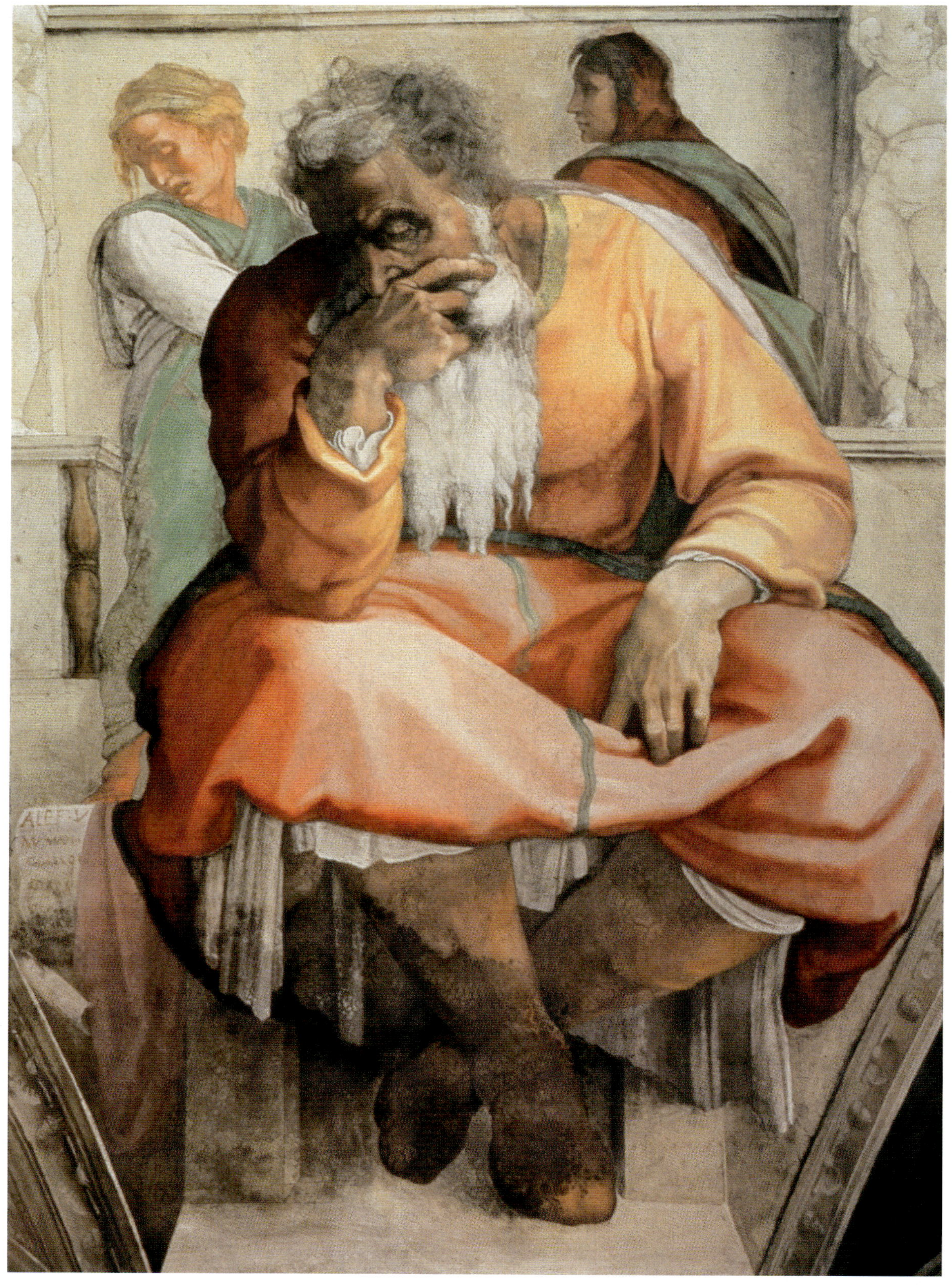

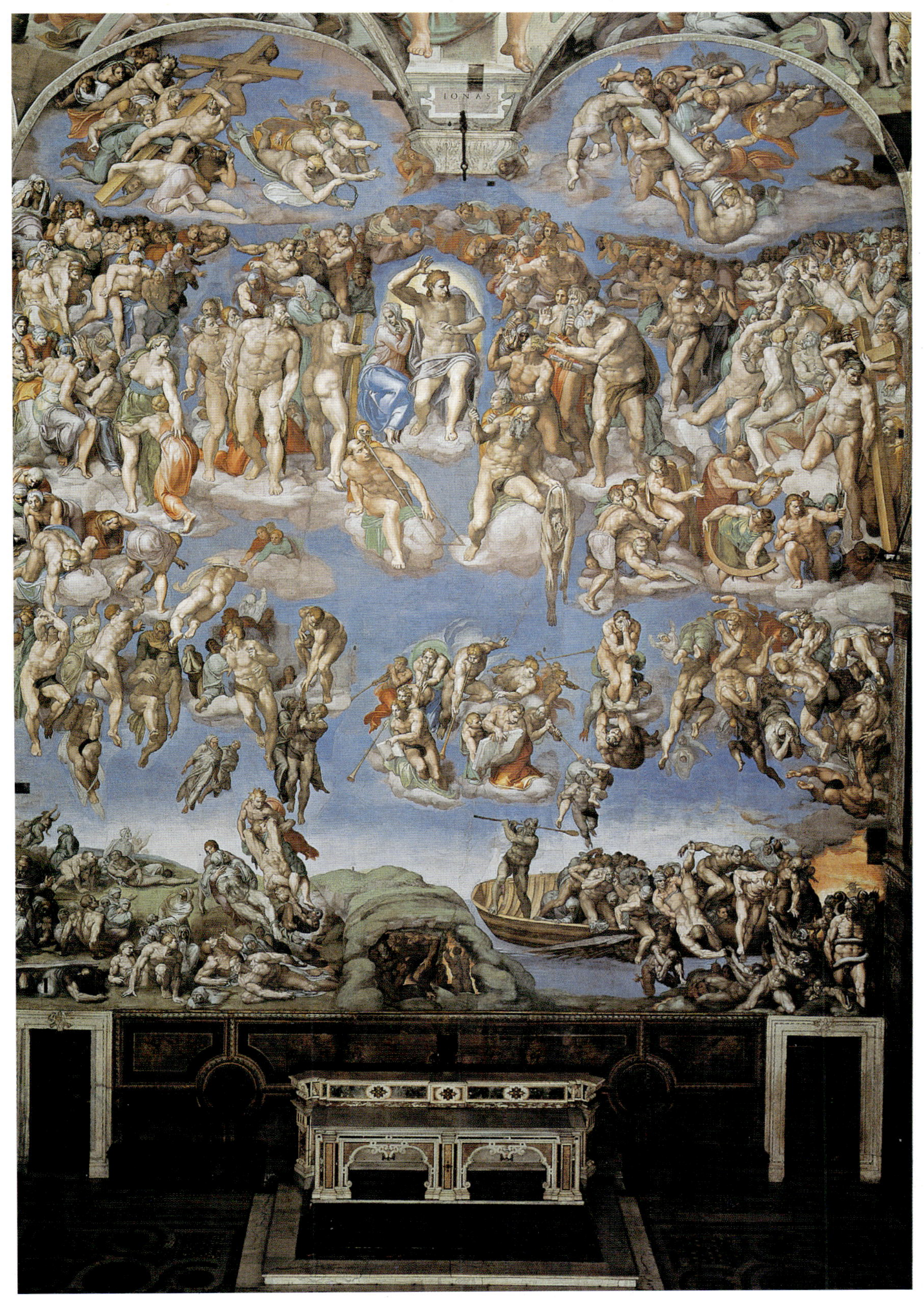

46. *The Prophet Jeremiah* (Lateral paintings of the Prophets), 1511. Fresco. Sistine Chapel, Vatican.

47. *The Last Judgment* (Full view), 1534-1541. Fresco. Sistine Chapel, Vatican.

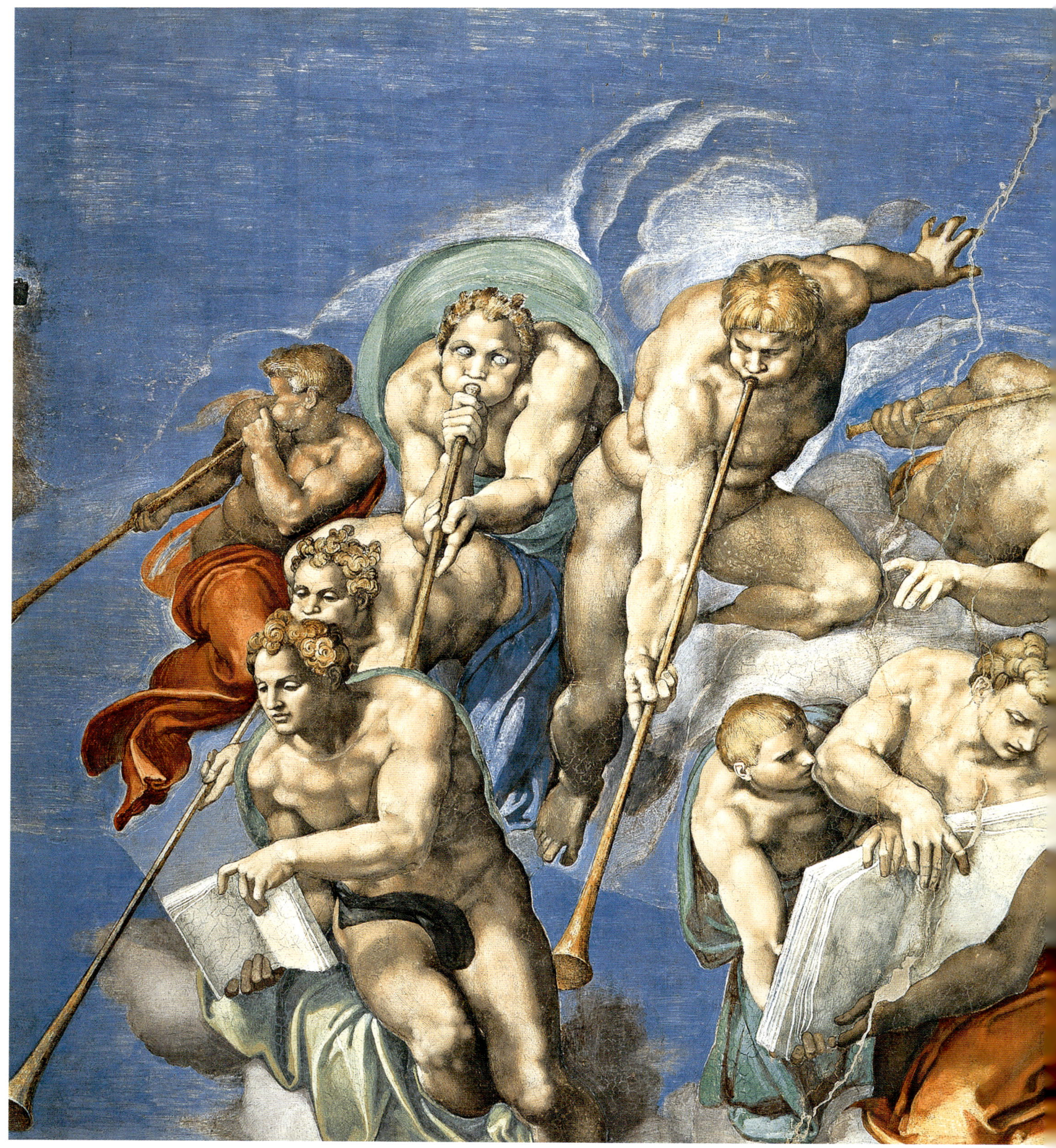

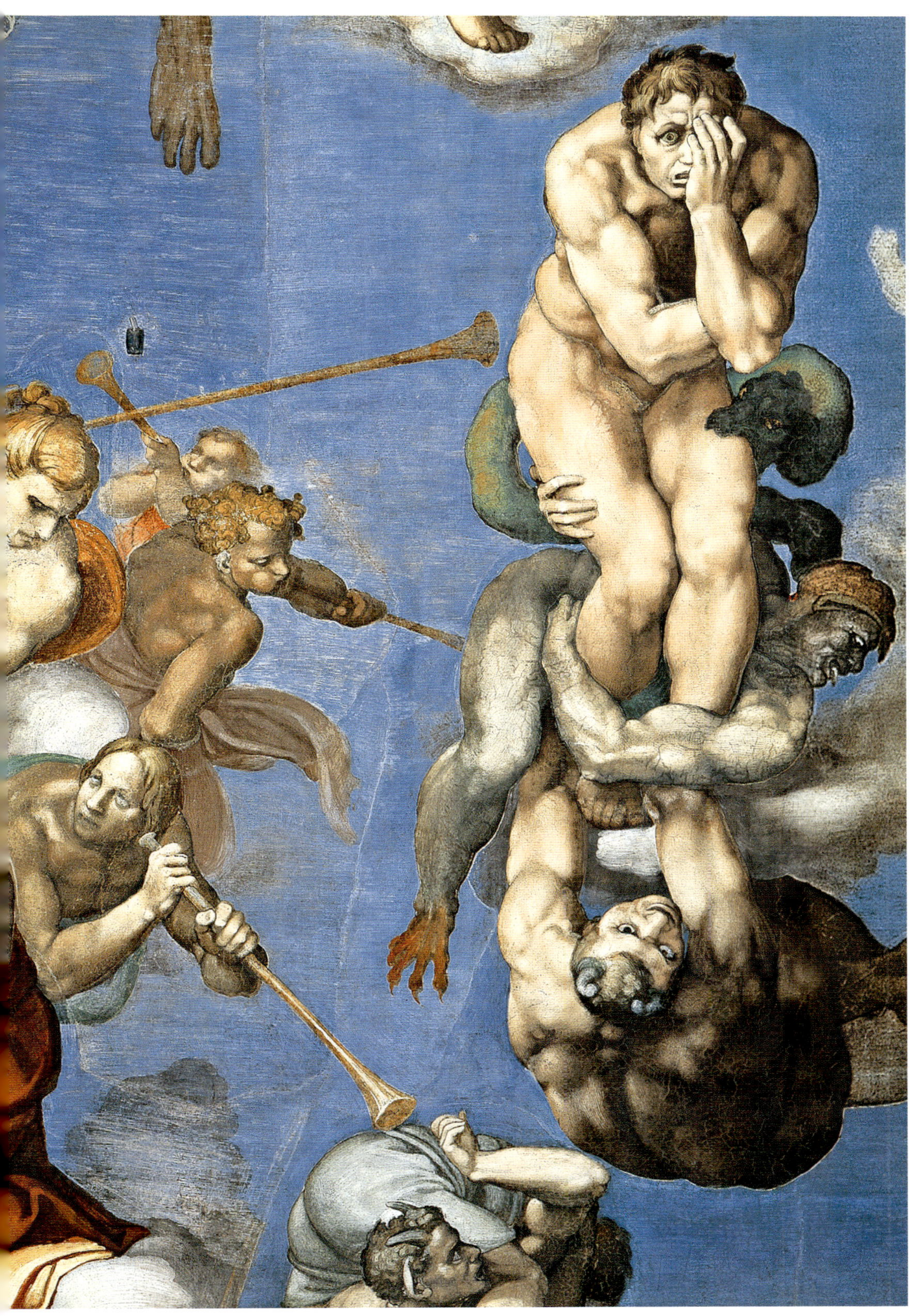

48. *The Angels Blowing the Trumpets of the Dead.* Detail of the *Last Judgement.* Fresco after restoration. Sistine Chapel, Vatican.

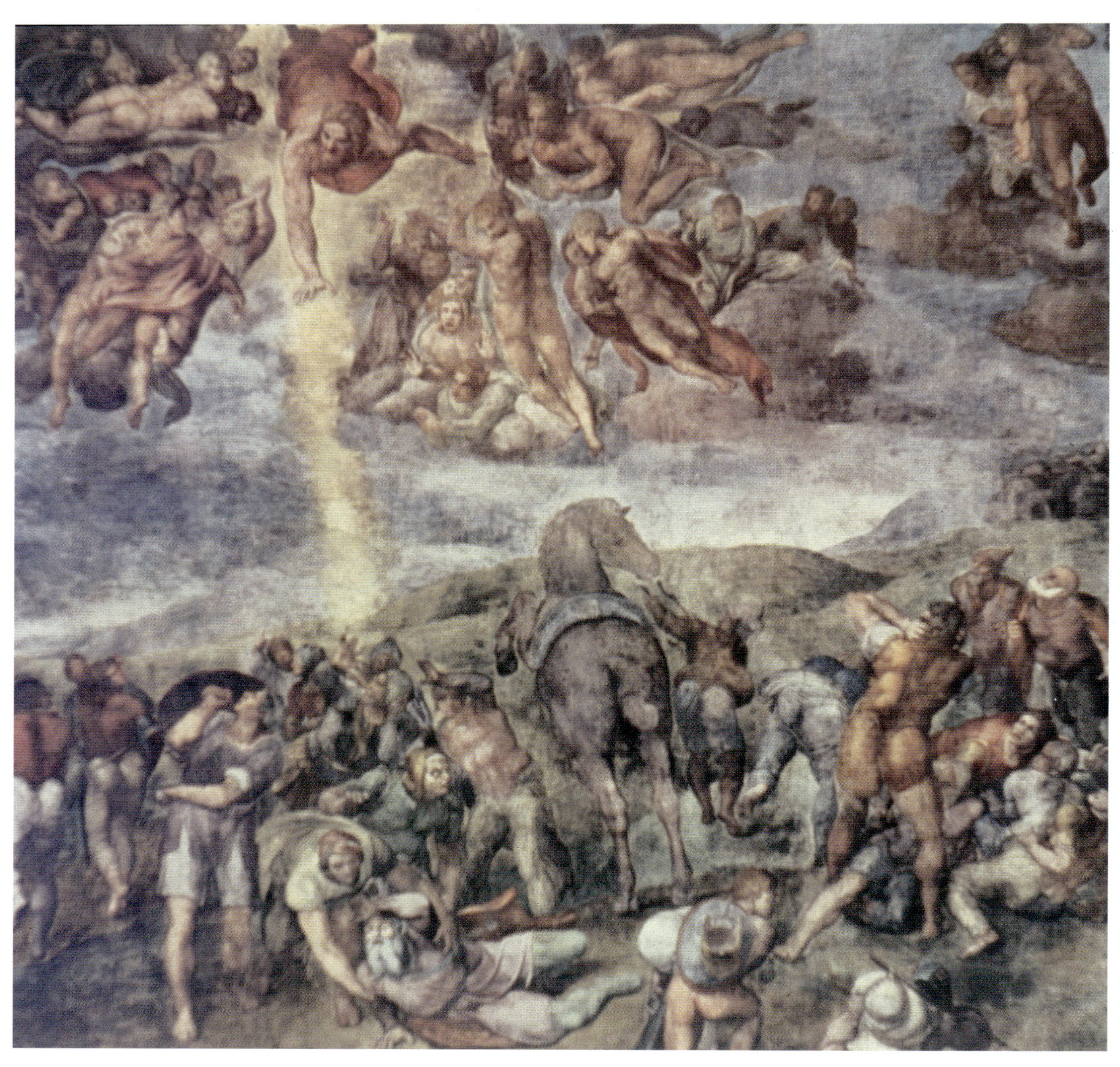

49. *The Conversion of St. Paul,* 1542-1545. Fresco, 624 x 661 cm. Pauline Chapel, Rome.

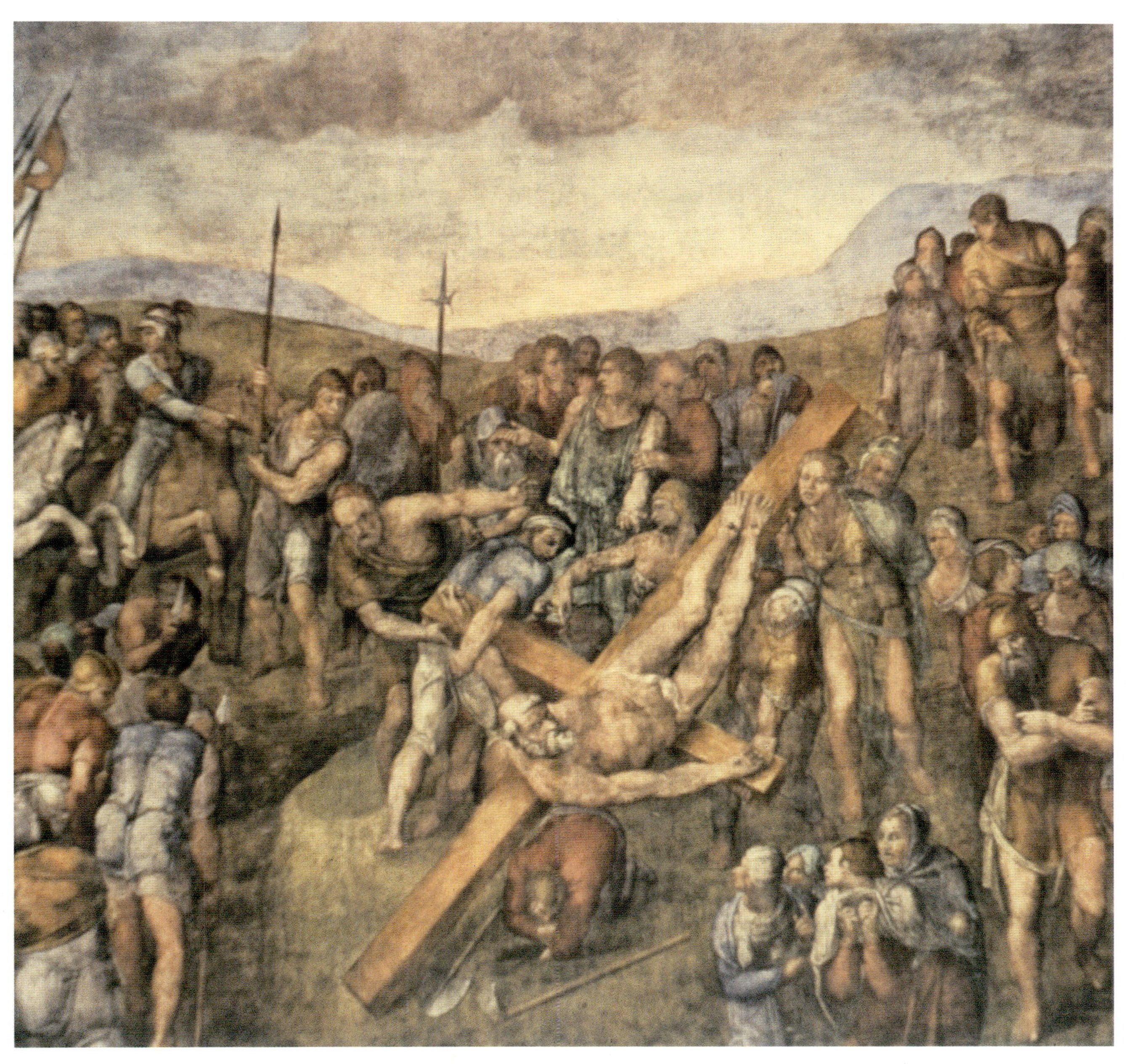

50. *Crucifixion of St. Peter,* 1546-1550. Fresco, 625 x 661 cm. Pauline Chapel, Rome.

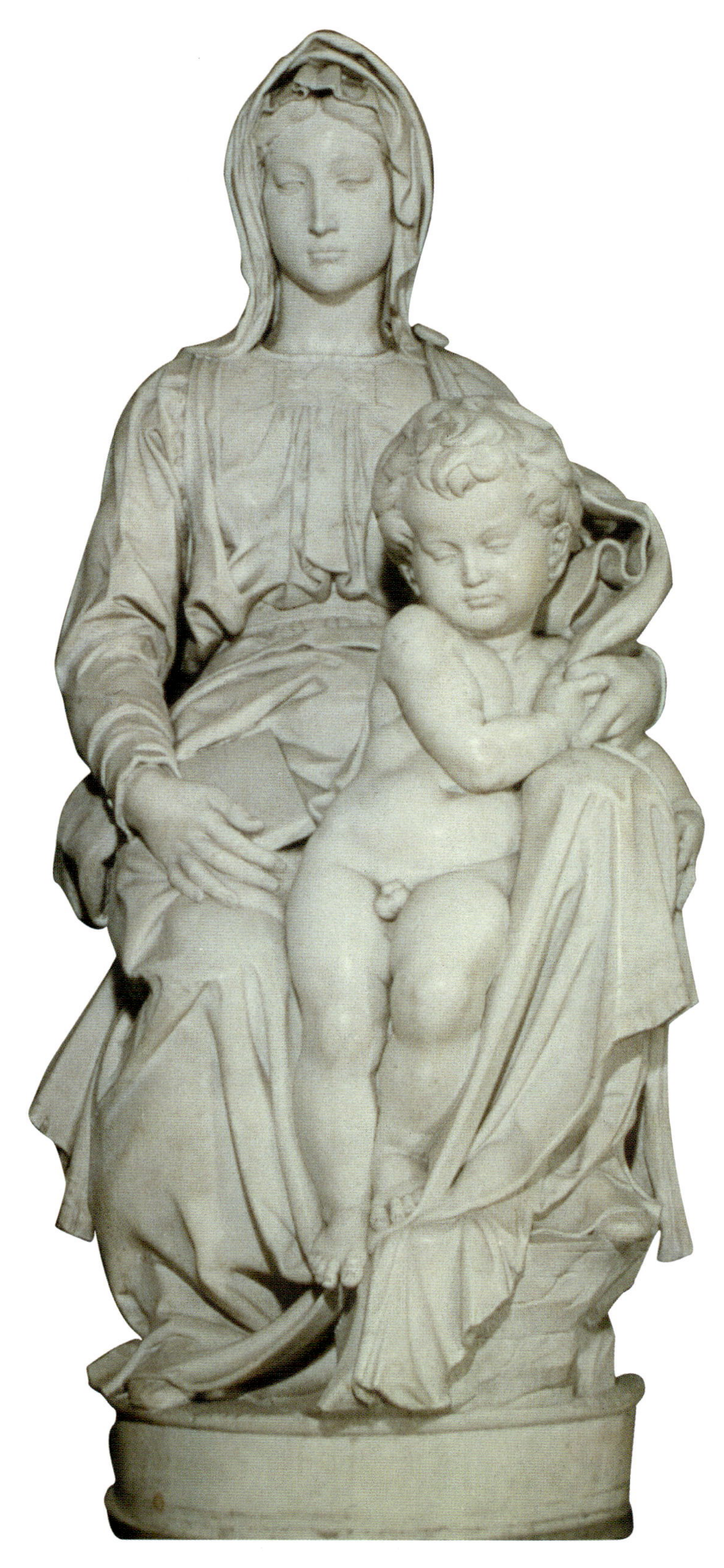

51. *Madonna and Child,*
1503-1506.
Marble, 121.9 cm.
Notre Dame, Bruges.

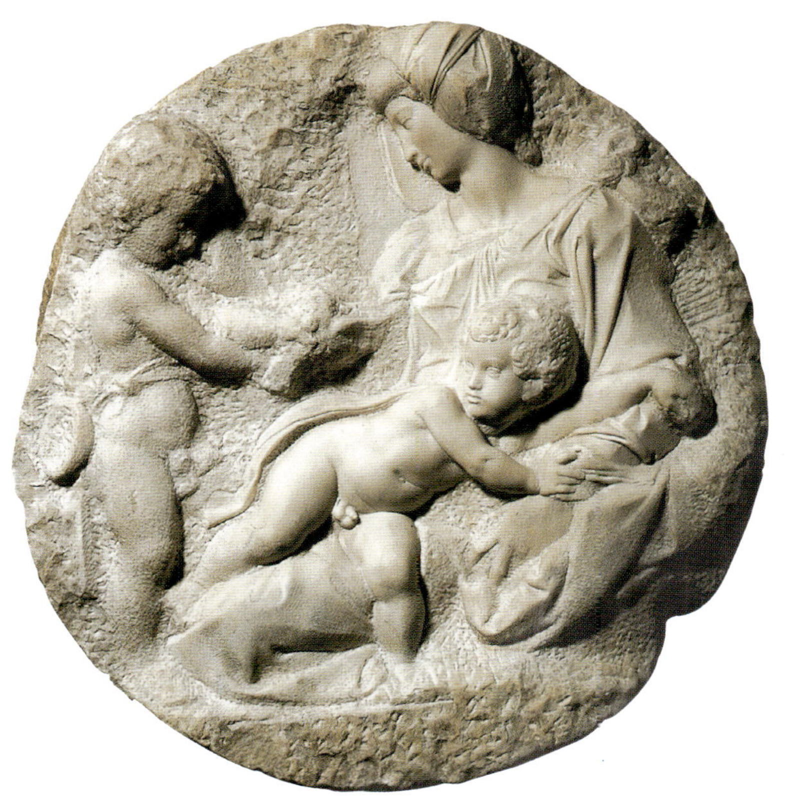

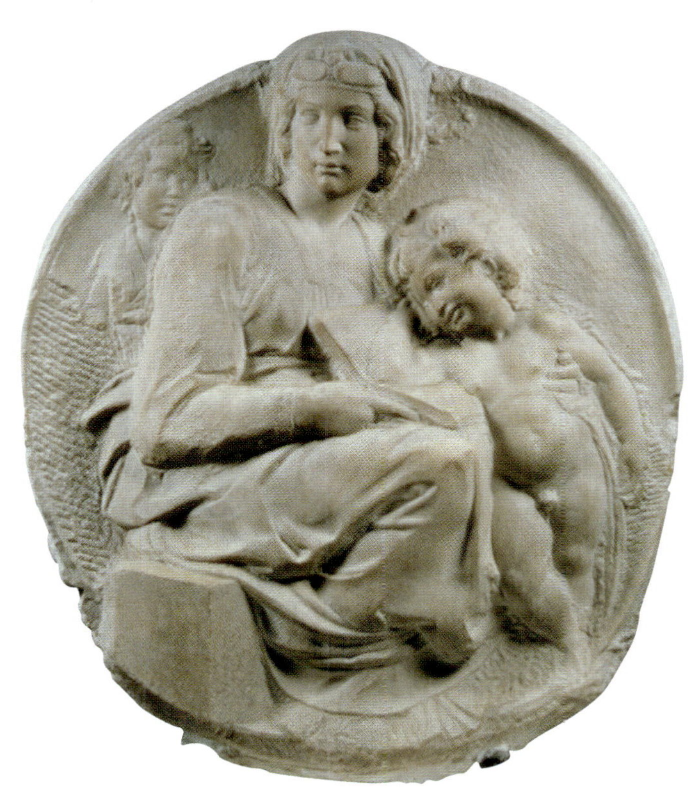

52. *Virgin with Child and Saint John the Baptist as a Child* or *Tondo Taddei*. Marble, 104 x 167cm. Royal Academy of Arts, London.

53. *The Pitti Madonna,* 1504-1505. Marble, 85 x 82.5 cm. Bargello, Florence.

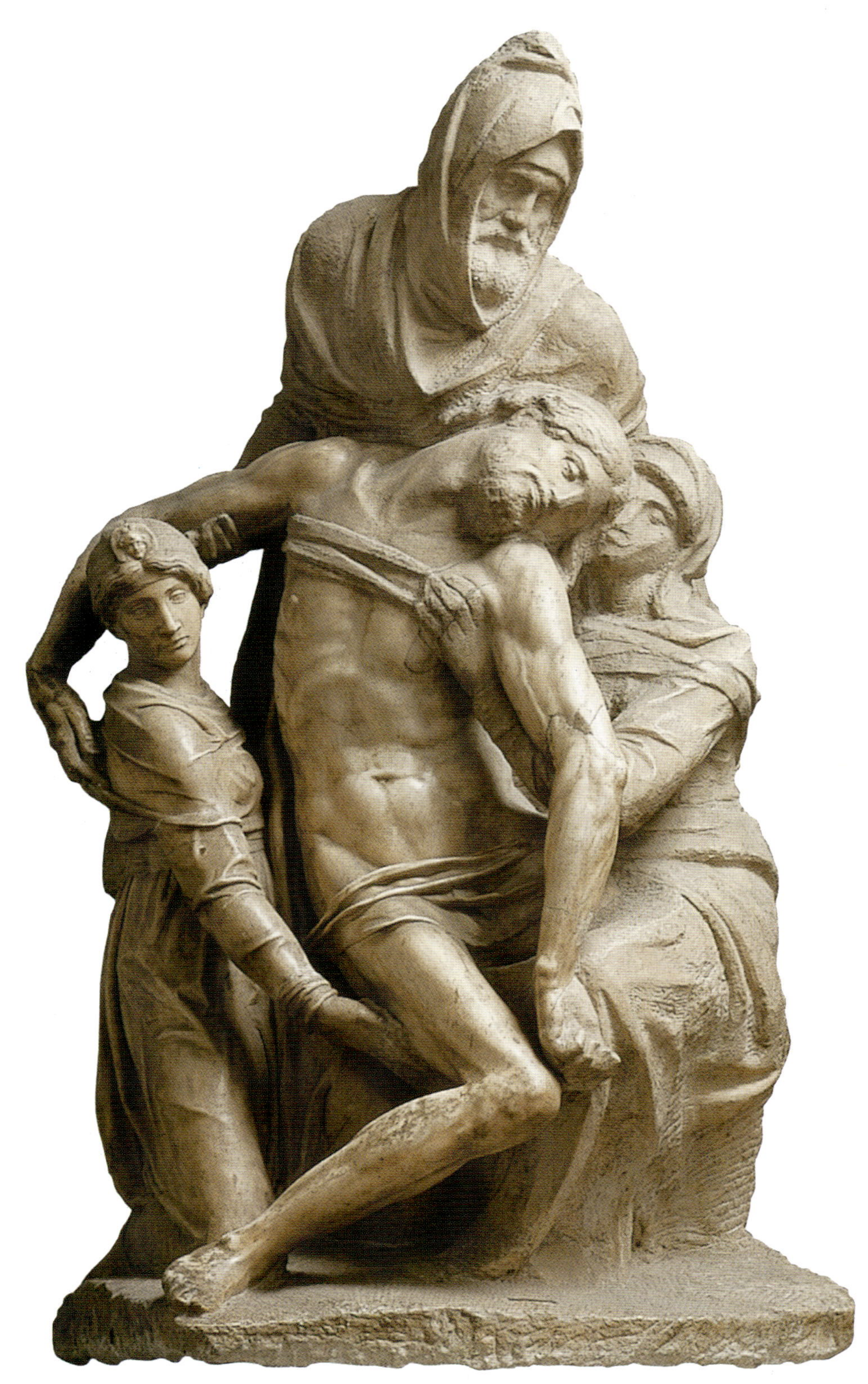

54. *Pietà de Florence*, 1547-1555. Marble, 226 cm. Museo dell'Opera del Duomo, Florence.

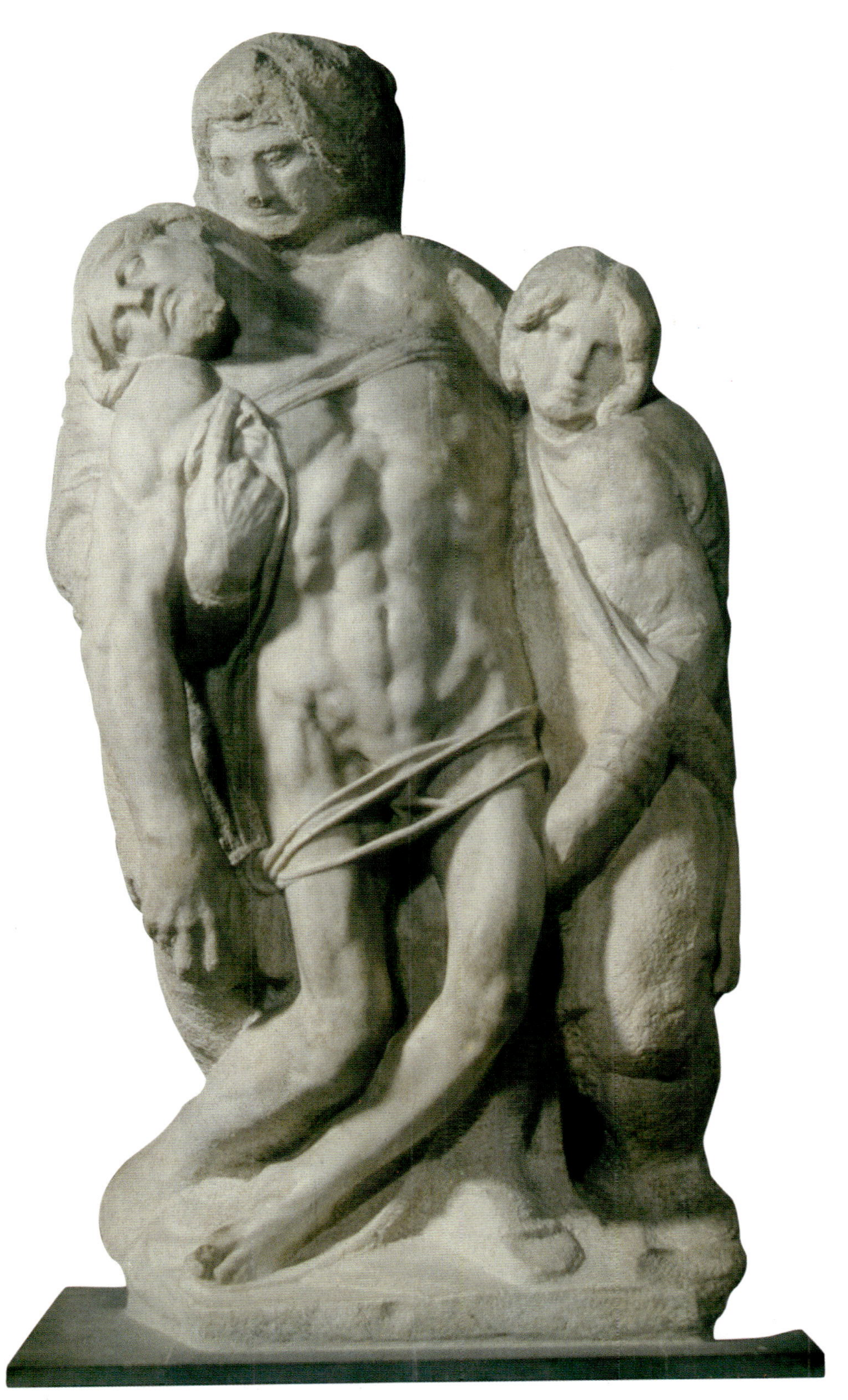

55. *Palestrina Pieta,* circa 1555. Marble, 253 cm. Accademia, Florence.

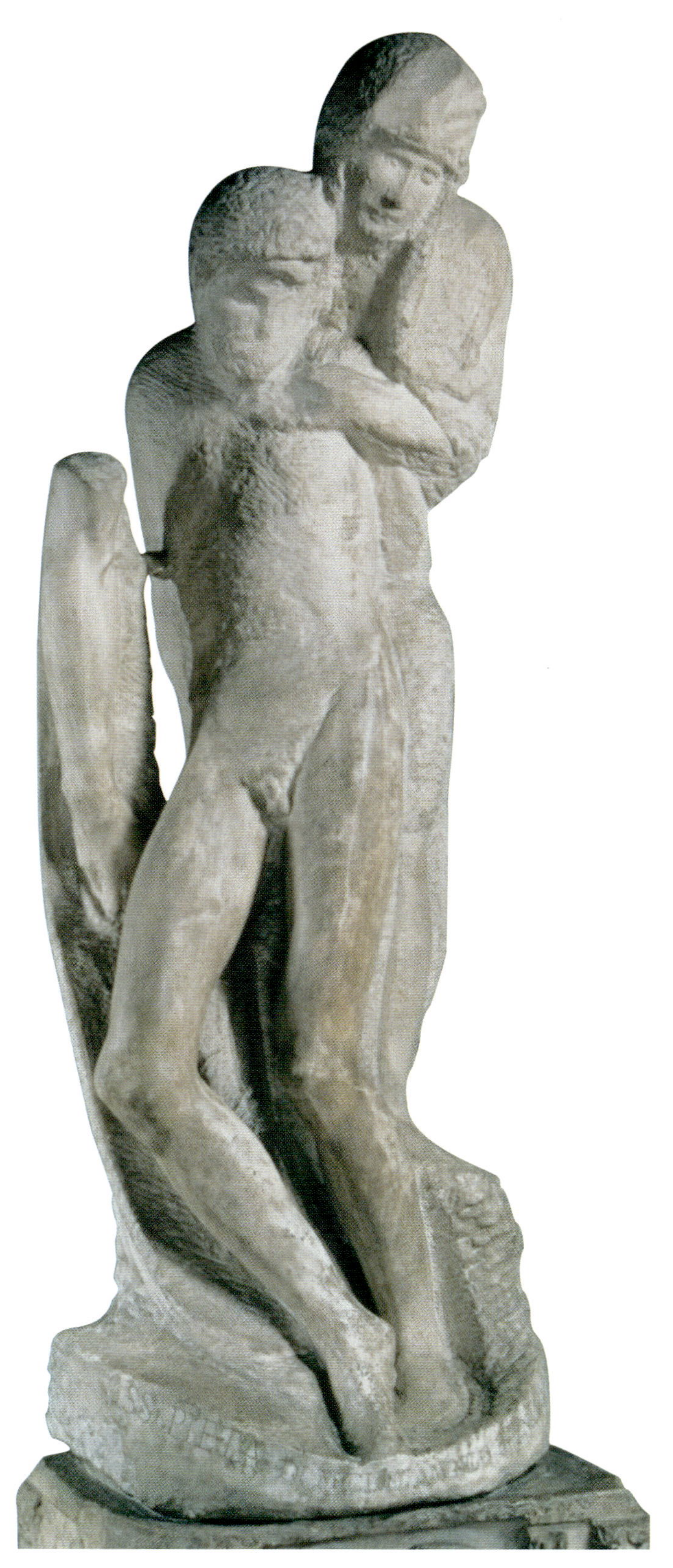

56. *The Rondanini Pieta,*
circa 1552-1564.
Marble, 195 cm.
Castello Sforzesco,
Milan.

The Sketch Artist

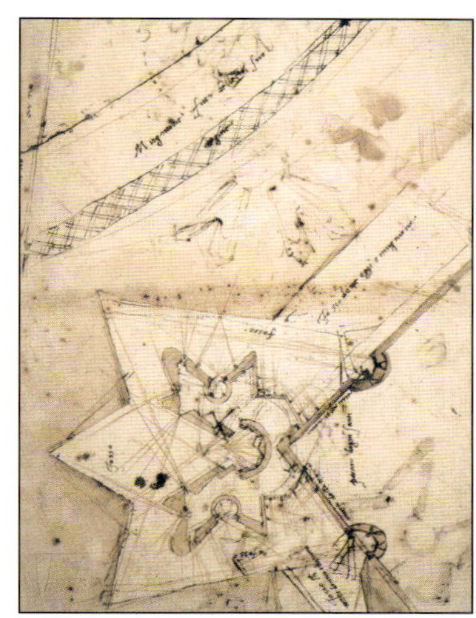

Sketching was always second nature to Michelangelo, but only as a necessary step in his quest for esthetic perfection and transcendence – never as an art form in its own right. From early childhood to old age, artistic ambition made him a prolific sketcher. We recall his time in the morgue, capturing human anatomy with a pen or pencil to obtain total purity and beauty in rendering each line of the body. For Michelangelo, drawing was a special way to jot down feelings, thoughts and impressions in order to communicate with himself. Today, through bequests, donations, exhibitions and family archives, Michelangelo's sketches can be seen across Europe in Florence, London, Oxford and the Louvre Museum in Paris.

A Most Exceptional Individual

In the following verse, written at age 76, Michelangelo offers a glimpse of the inner tensions that were always haunting him:

Such slavery and such concern
And such prejudice, and such imperilment
For my soul, to sculpt here things divine.

Ever the free soul, Michelangelo was also a man of duty. As a Humanist, his twofold message contained both Pagan values that inspired and freed his talent and Christian values that exalted and subjugated him. Yet this duality fostered works characterized by three inseparable components: (1) vigorous, sound and fully-rounded brushstrokes, (2) faces richly suggestive of inner depth and (3) a radiant passion for the raw human body and its dynamics in three-dimensional space. There is no shortage of writing on the sculptures of Michelangelo and his life's work as a textbook model of uniqueness – such as the case of Da Vinci. All stress that Michelangelo was a man with extraordinary stamina, a genius, an innovative artist and a creator of unprecedented wonders. As Giorgio Vasari once said of the talent, dazzle and effort he saw in his friend:

"His imagination was so powerful that his hands were incapable of executing the grand, terrible ideas his spirit conceived, so he often spoiled or abandoned works halfway through. And I know that, just before he died, he burnt countless sketches, drawings and portfolios so no one would ever see the difficulties his talent faced or all the effort that went into his accomplishments – so that no one would ever see him as less than perfect."

57. *Project for the strengthening of the Porta al Prato d'Ognissanti*, 1529. Quill and red chalk, 41 x 57 cm. Casa Buonarroti, Florence.

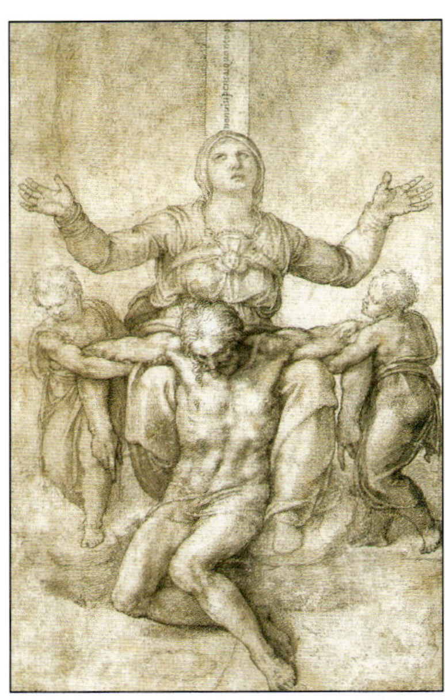

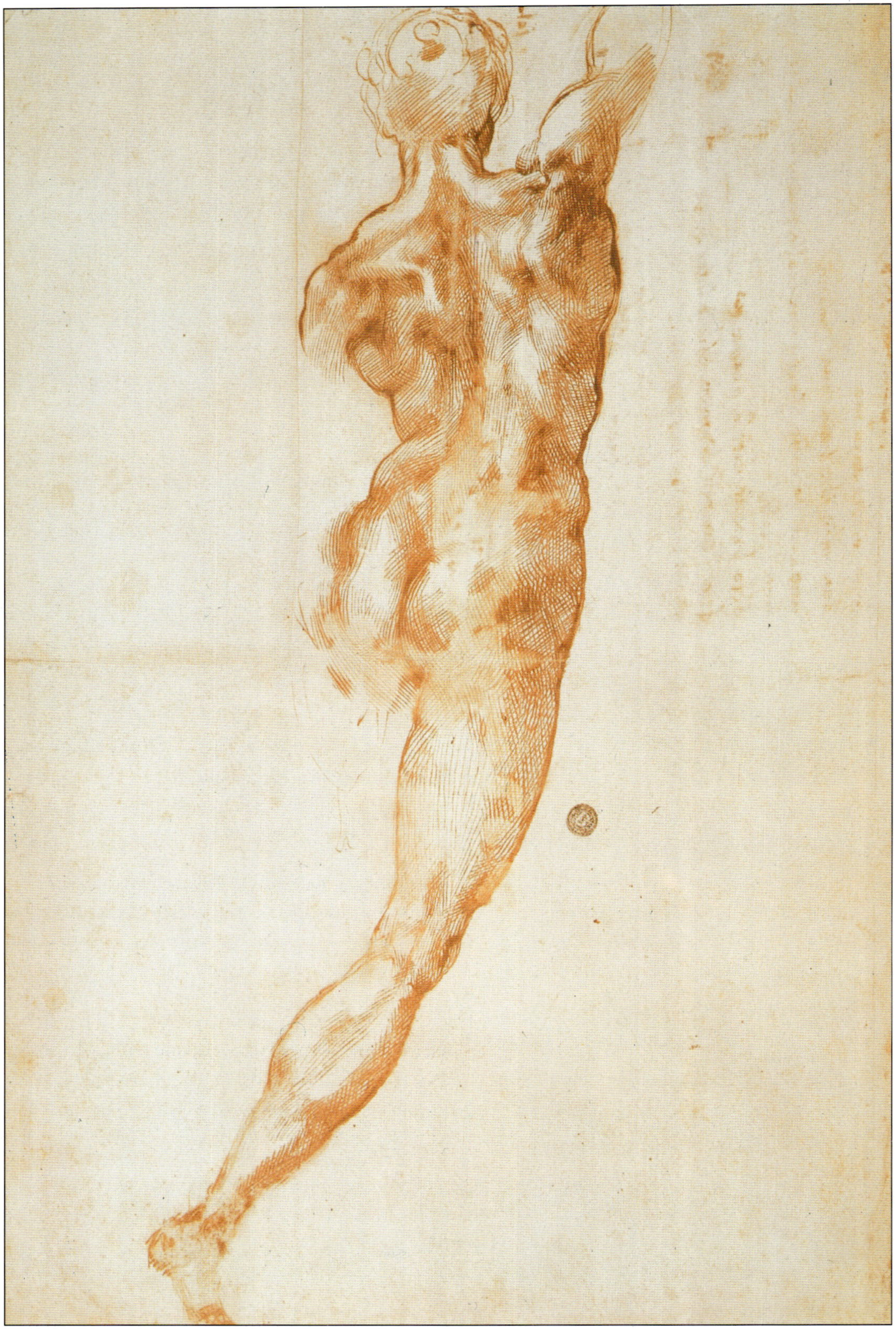

58. *Pietà*, 1538-1540.
Black stone,
29 x 19 cm.
Isabella Stewart
Gardner Museum,
Boston.

59. Nude Study for *The Battle of Cascina,* circa 1504. Quill, 40.8 x 28.4 cm. Casa Buonarotti, Florence.

60. Study for the *Libyan Sibyl,* 1511.
Red Chalk,
28.5 x 20.5 cm.
Metropolitan
Museum, New York.

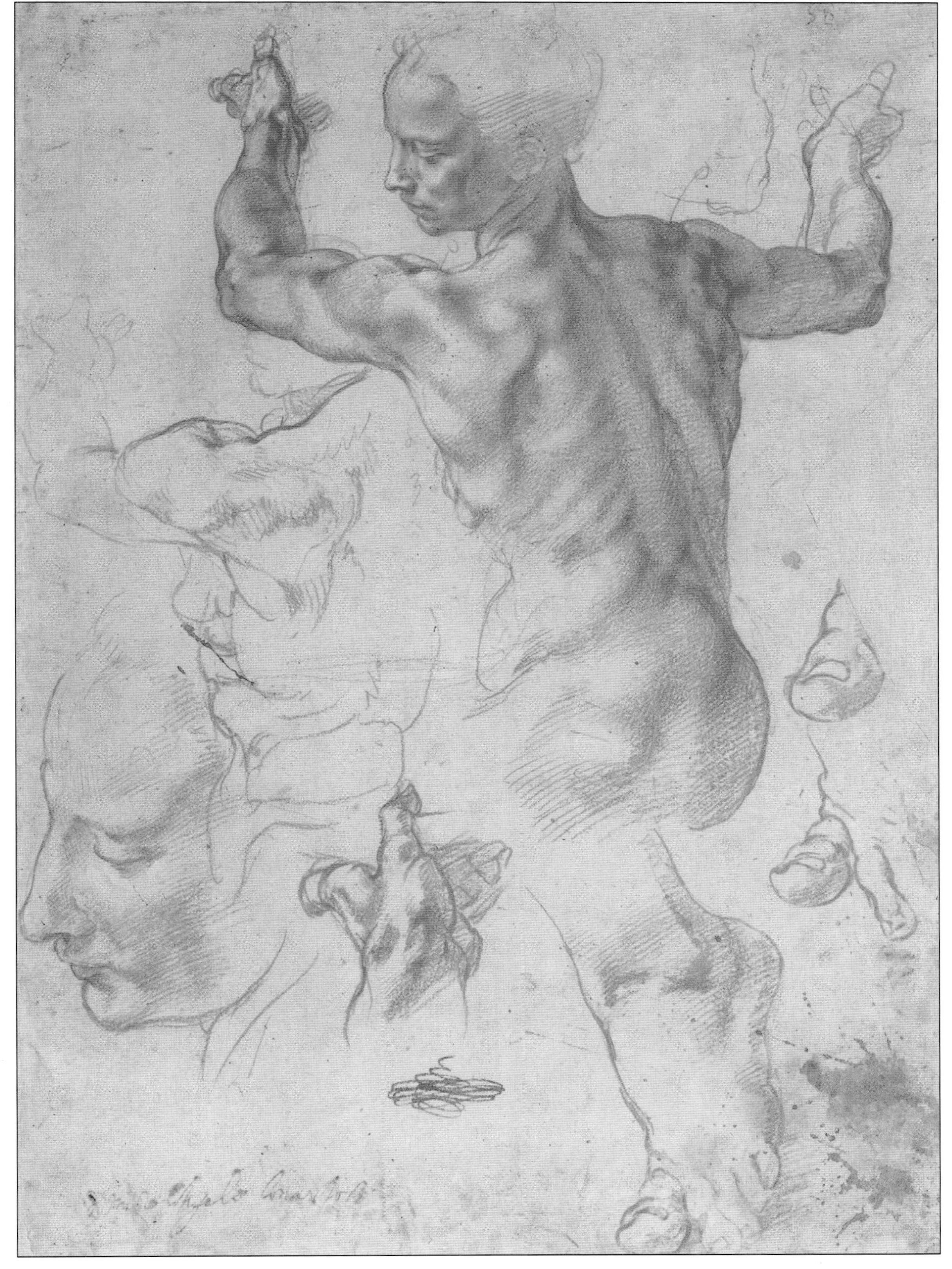

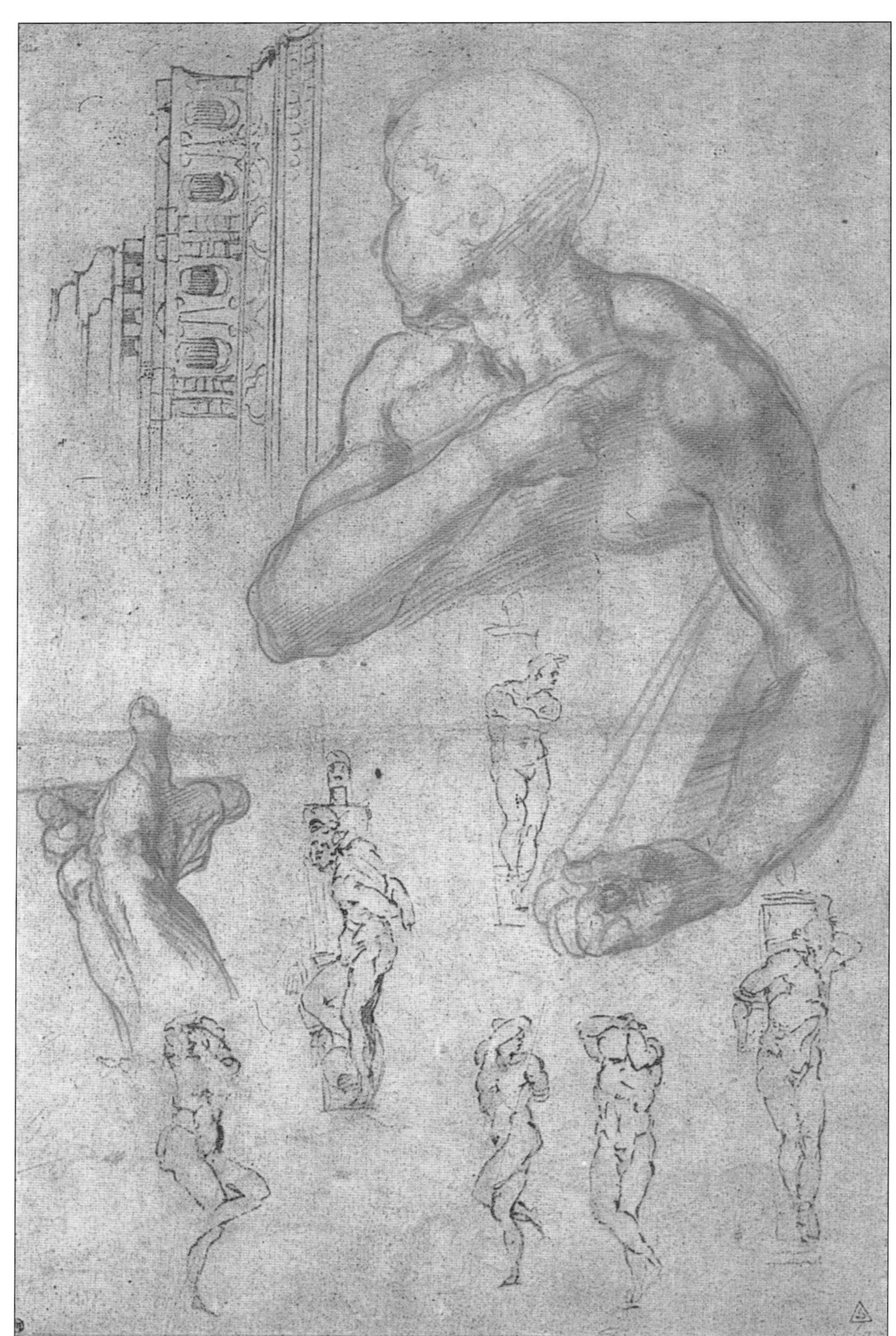

61. Study of a craftsman and the right hand of the Libyan Sibyl, six slaves, part of building. Red chalk on paper, feather and ink, 28.8 x 19.4 cm. Ashmolean Museum, Oxford.

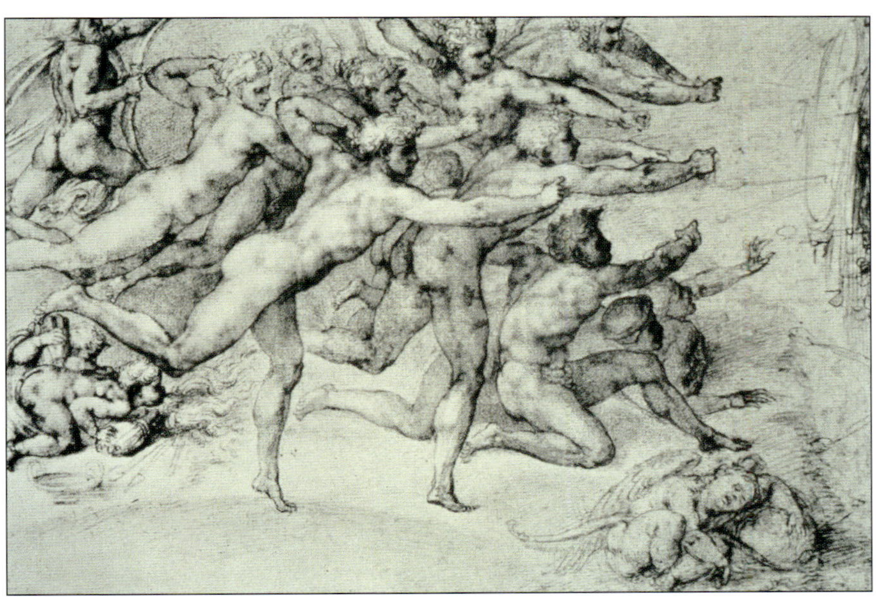

The pursuit of excellence haunted Michelangelo all his life, aggravated by an oversized ego and stamina superior to that of his contemporaries. Michelangelo often passed himself off as a self-taught artist owing little to anyone else. He dismissed any influence from Ghirlandaio and only barely admitted some from Bertoldo di Giovanni. Pretentious he was, but his originality was real nonetheless. And he had no noteworthy students. At best he swapped ideas on creativity, but only with Giorgio Vasari. In addition to any artistic inspiration from these exchanges, Vasari teamed up with Ascavio Condivi to help Michelangelo write his autobiography.

Though physically strong, Michelangelo was an ugly man with a broken nose dating from a childhood brawl. He cultivated a taste for suffering, quite possibly as a path to redemption. That he never found love tortured him and drove him to despair. In the safety of solitude, he cultivated what Jean Destrenes terms "the culture of bitterness". Running into Raphael in the corridors of the Vatican one day, Michelangelo lashed out, "You're strutting around with your courtiers, just like a prince." And his last days were gloomy indeed, heavily strained by personal feuds and attacks on his already timeless artwork.

At all events, no one questions the genius in Michelangelo. All rank him above Caravaggio, Da Vinci, Raphael, Titian and Veronese, if only because his works ranged from drawing to sculpture (Da Vinci never carved) and painting, plus architecture, urban planning and army engineering. Michelangelo's works just have to look at you *once* to find you. Beyond the contemplation they entice, take communion with them as the artist so intimately intended.

62. *The Archers Shooting at a Herm*, circa 1531. Red chalk, 21.5 x 32 cm. Royal Library, Windsor.

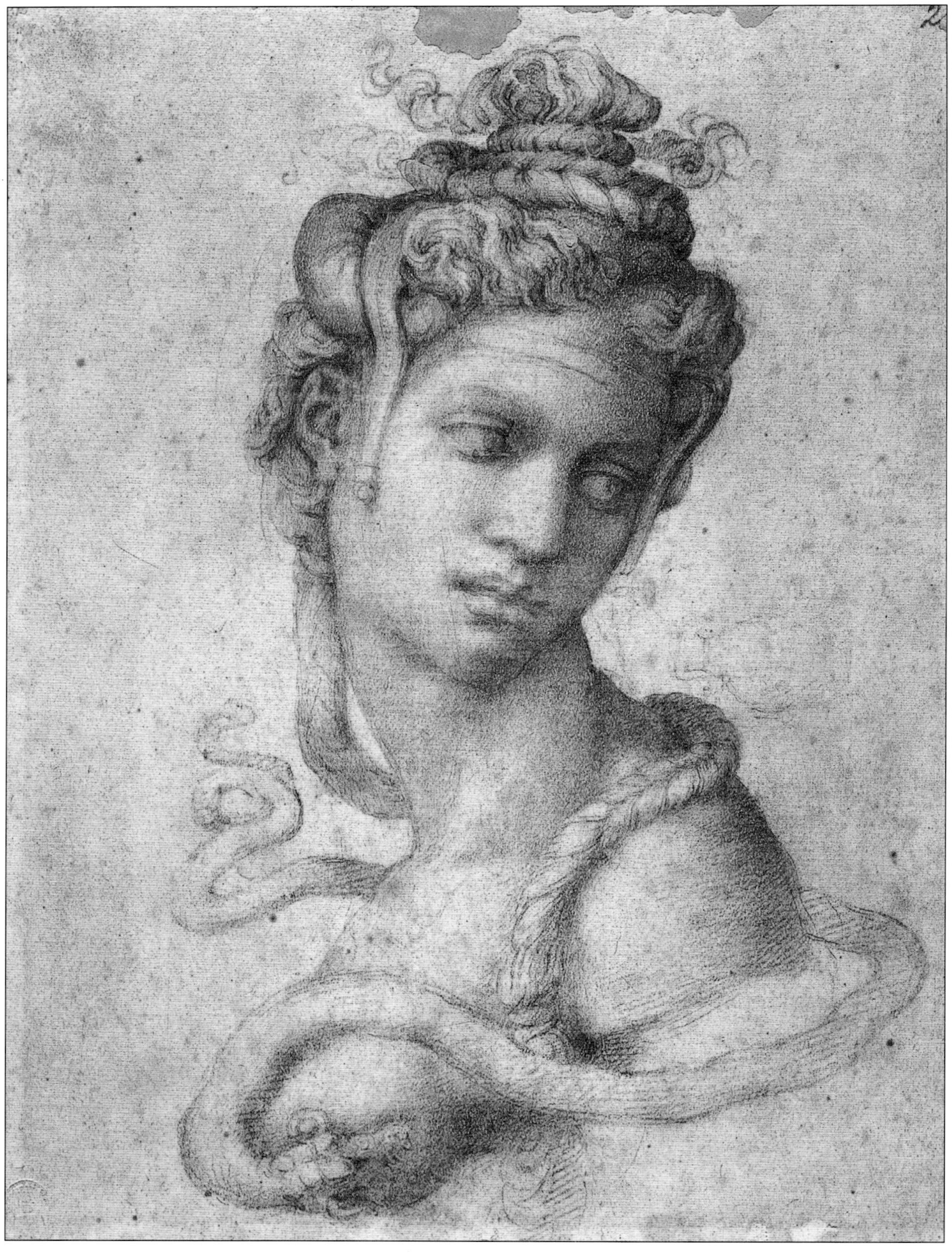

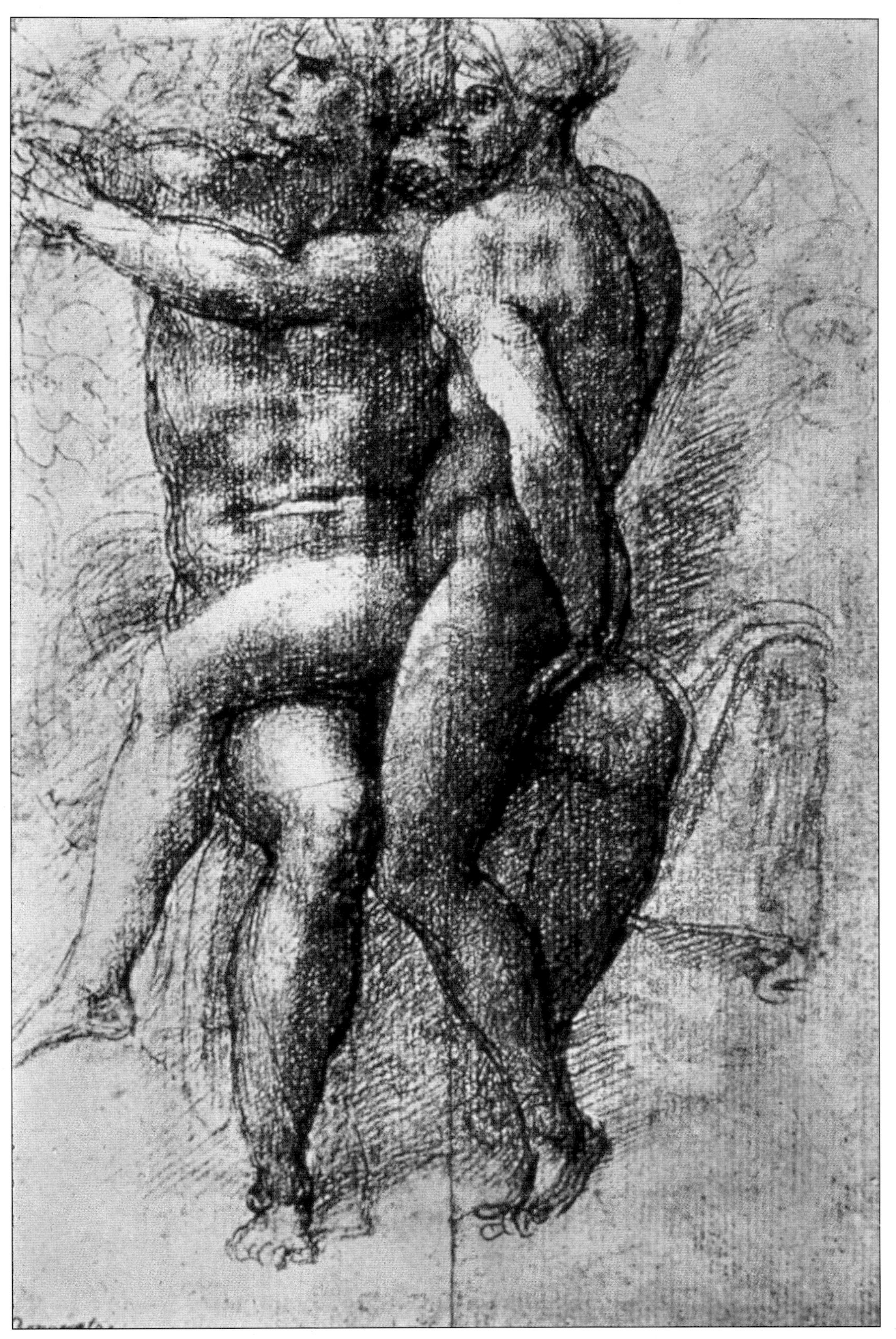

63. Copy from Michelangelo, *Bustle of Cleopatra, circa 1532.* Black chalk on paper, 26 x 20.5 cm. Casa Buonarotti, Florence.

64. *Nude study* for Sistine Chapel Ceiling, 1511. Red chalk, 29.7 x 21.4 cm. Teyler Museum, Haarlem.

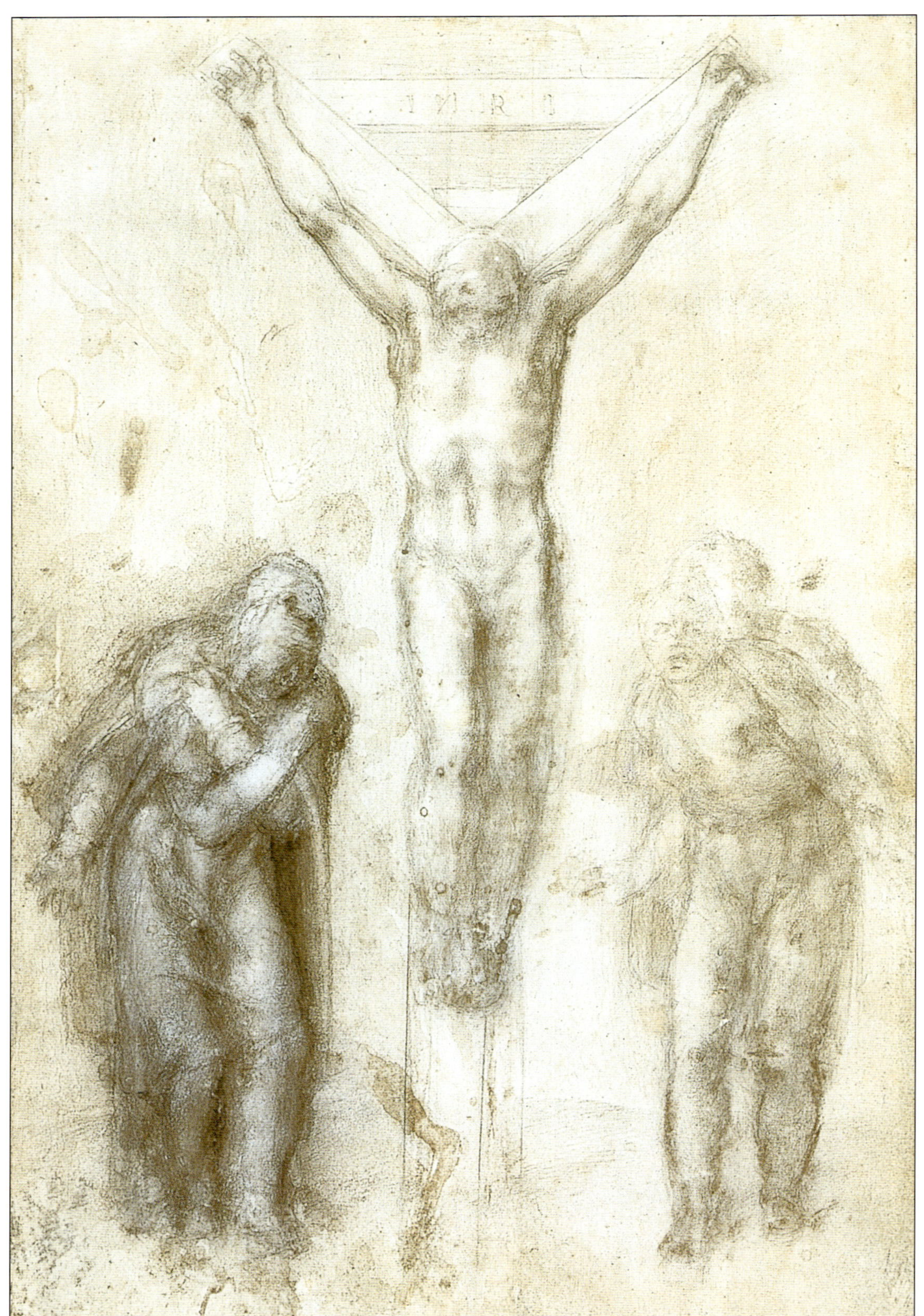

65. *Crucifixion with the Virgin Mary and Saint John*, circa 1550-1555. Charcoal touched up with white pigment and grey water-colour, 41.5 x 28.5 cm. British Museum, London.

BIOGRAPHY

1475 Born on March 6th in Caprese, Tuscany, second child to Lodovico di Leonardo Buonarroti Simoni and Francesca di Neri di Miniato del Sera.

1481 Enrollment Francesco da Urbino's Latin school following his mother's death.

1483 Birth of rival Raphael Sanzio in Urbino.

1484 Start of a three-year apprenticeship under Domenico Ghirlandaio.

1485 Stays with Bertoldo in the Medici gardens near San Marco where he studies its ancient and contemporary works of sculpture.

1486 Death of Lorenzo de Medici; completion of *Battle of the (Lapiths and) Centaurs, Madonna of the Stairs* (a.k.a. *Madonna of the Steps*) and a wooden crucifix for Santo Spirito in Florence.

1487 Flight to Venice and Bologna as the armies of Charles VIII threaten to take over Florence and rumours predict the imminent fall of the Medici.

1488 Arrival in Rome to become a protégé of Jacopo Galli, who commissions his *Bacchus*; completion of *Sleeping Cupid*, now lost.

1489 Commission from Cardinal Jean de la Grolaye de Villiers for the *Rome Pietà*.

1490 Death of Cardinal Bilhères shortly after completion of the *Rome Pietà*.

1491 Altarpiece for Sant'Agostino in Rome as King Louis XII of France invades Italy.

1492 Return to Florence and commission for *David* in marble.

1493 Commission for statues of the Twelve Apostles slated for the cathedral dome in Florence – only sketches for St. Matthew were ever completed; death of the 25-day Pope Pius III; election of Pope Julius II; commission for the *Bruges Madonna*; completion of *Taddei Tondo* and *Pitti Tondoi*.

1494 Completion and inauguration of *David* at Piazza dei Signori; portfolio work for *Battle of Cascina*.

1495 Commission from Julius II for his tomb in Rome and the start of stormy relations with the Vatican; subsequent stay in Carrara to secure the marble needed.

1496 Return to Florence

1497 Execution of *Doni Tondo* for Agnolo Doni (possibly completed within 1503 to 1505)

1498 Arrival in Rome to paint the Sistine ceiling.

1499 Start of decoration work for the Stanze of the Vatican, concurrent with the Sistine worksite.

1512 Unveiling of the new Sistine ceiling.

1513 Death of Pope Julius II and election of Leo X, son of Lorenzo de Medici; renegotiation of the contract for the tomb of Julius II.

1515 Leo X dubs Michelangelo Count Palatino.

1516 Return to Florence; commission from Leo X for the façade of San Lorenzo there.

1520 First drawings for the Medici Chapel.

1521 Death of Leo X (Giovanni de Medici) and election of Hadrian VI; Michelangelo receives no Vatican commissions and works on the Medici family tombs.

1523 Election of Clement VII (Giulio de'Medici)

1524 Start of *Dusk* and *Dawn* for the tomb of Lorenzo de Medici and a commission for the Laurentian Library.

1527 Sack of Rome; flight of the Medici.

1528 Almost one year of army engineering, urban planning and architecture to defend Florence from the Medici.

1529 Appointment as army engineer in the Nove della Milizia, the nine-man military leadership of the Florentine armed forces.

1530 The Medici retake Florence; commission from the Duke of Ferrara for *Leda and the Swan* – highly acclaimed and now lost; execution work on the Medici chapel.

1531 *Noli me Tangere* portfolio.

1534 Final goodbye to Florence; death of Pope Clement VII and election of Paul III who commissions *Last Judgment*; permanent residence in Rome.

1536 Start of *Last Judgment* for the Sistine Chapel.

1538 Completion of working drawings to install the statue of Marcus Aurelius in Campidoglio.

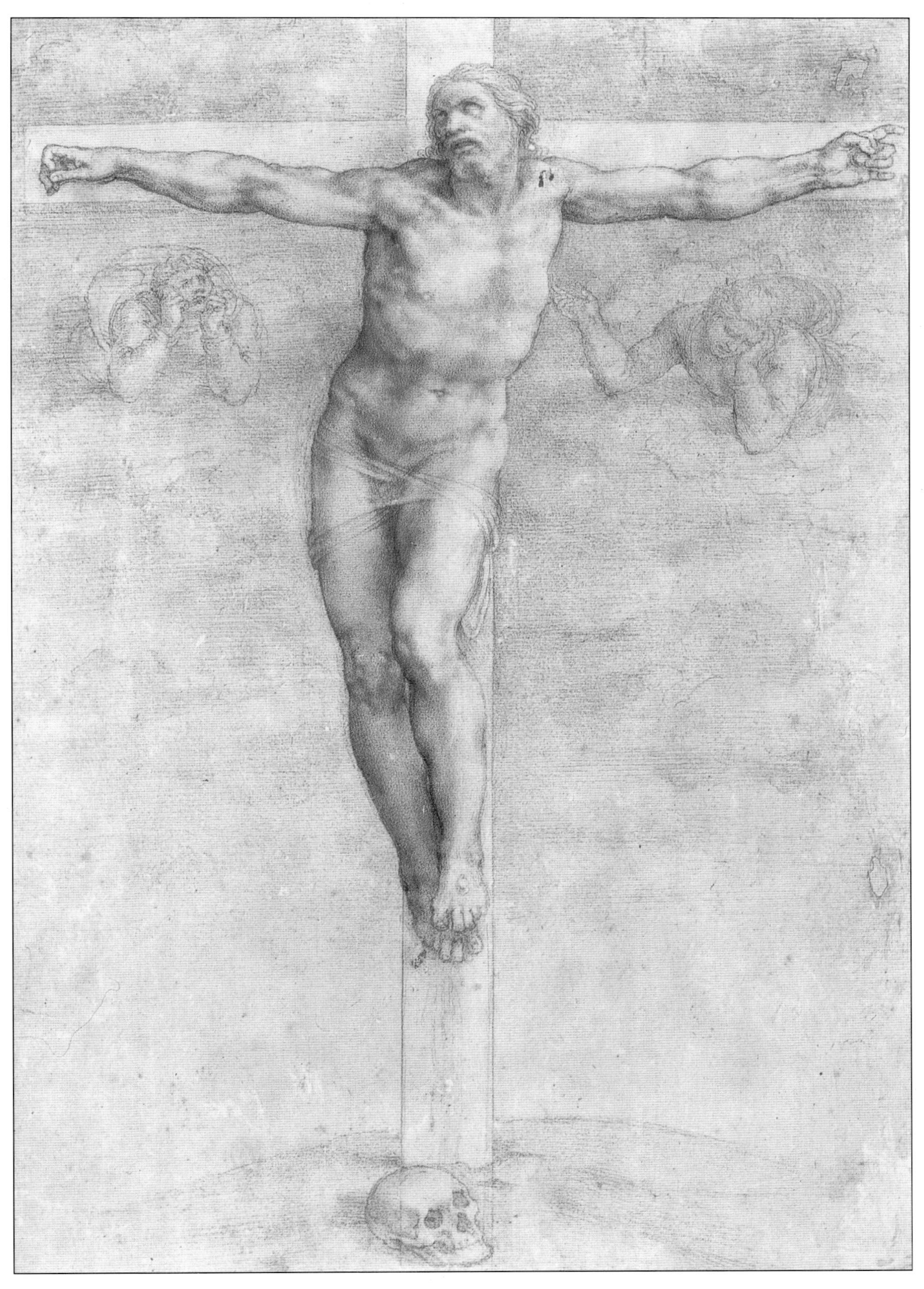

66. *Crucifixion,* circa 1540. Charcoal, 37 x 27 cm. British Museum, London.

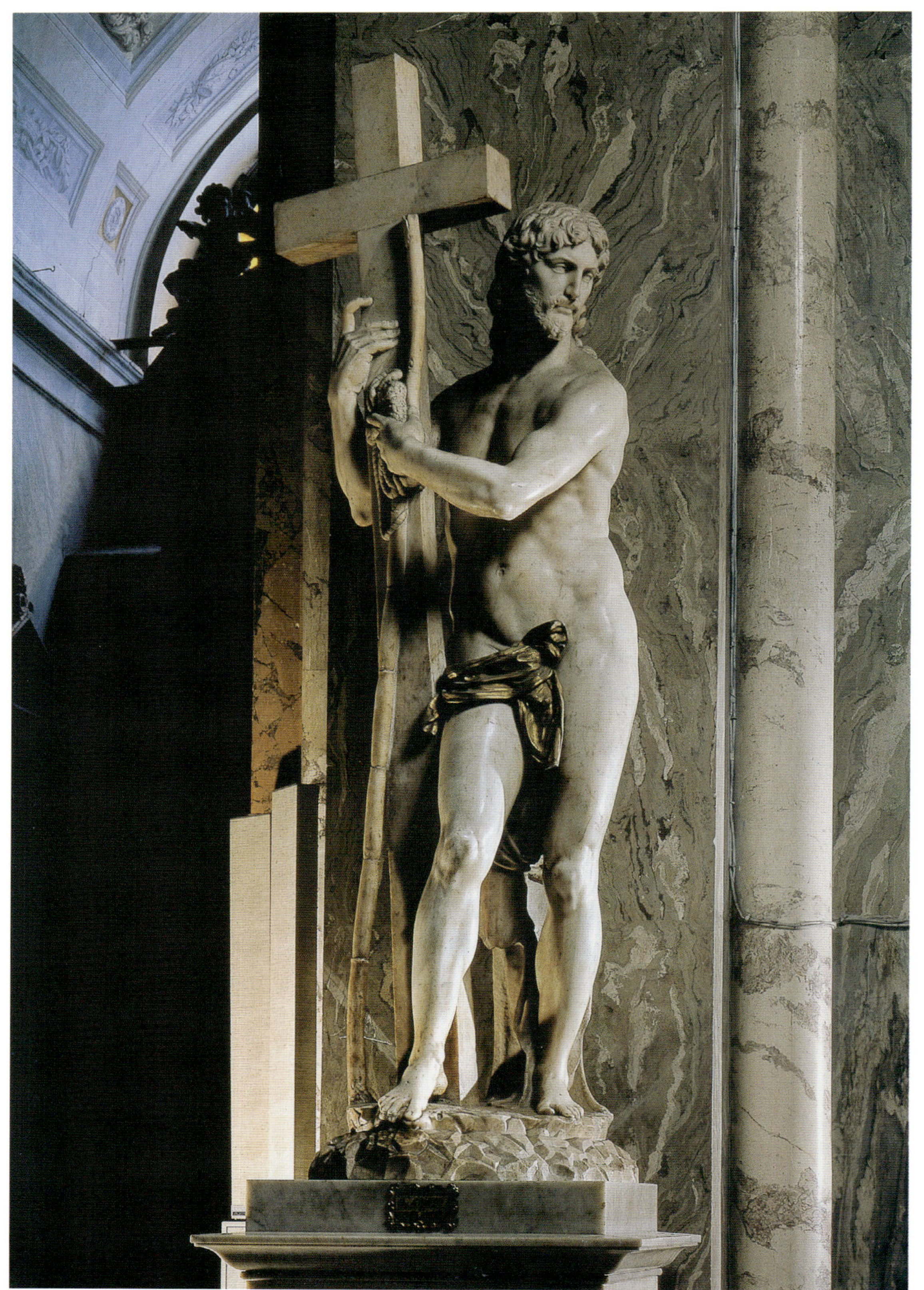

67. *Christ Ressurected,* 1518-1520. Marble. Santa Maria sopra Minerva, Rome.

1541 Inauguration of the *Last Judgment*.

1542 Worksite start-up for the Pauline Chapel.

1545 Completion of the tomb for Pope Julius II, one of Michelangelo's most time-consuming achievements.

1546 Appointment as chief architect to St. Peter's in Rome; work on St. Peter's and the Farnese Palace.

1547 Death of Vittoria Colonna, longtime friend and accomplished poetess, whom he met while working on the *Last Judgment*.

1549 Death of Paul III and election of Julius III; reconfirmation of the artist's commissions.

1550 Completion of the Pauline Chapel frescoes; start of the *Florentine Pietà*.

1552 Completion of the Capitoline stair.

1555 Death of Julius III, followed by Marcel II and Paul IV; reconfirmation of his appointment as chief architect of St. Peter's.

1556 Flight to Spoleta from Rome, now under threat from the Spanish Army.

1560 Drawings commissioned by Catherine de Medici to glorify her husband, King Henry II of France; design of a tomb for Giangiacomo de'Medici di Marignano and drawings for the *Porta Pia* – a hectic year.

1563 Appointment by Cosimo de Medici as "head" of his newly-founded Accademia in Florence.

1564 Council of Trent orders moralistic touch-ups to the *Last Judgment*; dies at home in Macel de Corvi three weeks later on February 18, 1564 of a "slow fever", as Vasari tells us.

LIST OF ILLUSTRATIONS